In a Pickle

Books by Jerry Apps

Fiction:

The Travels of Increase Joseph
In a Pickle

Nonfiction:

The Land Still Lives
Cabin in the Country
Barns of Wisconsin
Mills of Wisconsin and the Midwest
Breweries of Wisconsin
One-Room Country Schools
Wisconsin Traveler's Companion
Country Wisdom
Cheese: The Making of a Wisconsin Tradition
When Chores Were Done
Country Ways and Country Days
Humor from the Country
The People Came First: A History of Cooperative Extension
Ringlingville USA
Every Farm Tells a Story
Living a Country Year

Audio Books:

The Back Porch and Other Stories

Children's Books:

Eat Rutabagas
Stormy
Tents, Tigers, and the Ringling Brothers

In a Pickle

A Family Farm Story

Jerry Apps

Terrace Books
A trade imprint of the University of Wisconsin Press

Terrace Books, a trade imprint of the University of Wisconsin Press,
takes its name from the Memorial Union Terrace, located at
the University of Wisconsin–Madison. Since its inception in 1907,
the Wisconsin Union has provided a venue for students, faculty, staff,
and alumni to debate art, music, politics, and the issues of the day.
It is a place where theater, music, drama, literature, dance, outdoor activities,
and major speakers are made available to the campus and the community.
To learn more about the Union, visit www.union.wisc.edu.

Terrace Books
A trade imprint of the University of Wisconsin Press
1930 Monroe Street, 3rd Floor
Madison, Wisconsin 53711-2059

www.wisc.edu/wisconsinpress/

3 Henrietta Street
London WC2E 8LU, England

3   5   4   2

Printed in the United States of America

Library of Congress Cataloging-in-Publication Data
Apps, Jerold W., 1934–
In a pickle: a family farm story / Jerry Apps.
        p.   cm.
ISBN 0-299-22300-0 (cloth: alk. paper)
1. Family farms—Wisconsin—Waushara County—Fiction.
2. Farm life—Wisconsin—Waushara County—Fiction.
3. Pickle Industry—Wisconsin—Fiction.   I. Title.
        PS3601.P67I5   2007
        813´.6—dc22   2007011563

ISBN 0-299-22304-3 (pbk.: alk. paper)

Contents

Contents

Acknowledgments

Several years ago I was having dinner with my daughter, Sue. She suggested the idea for this book, having heard my "pickle factory" stories since she was a little girl. Sue, who is now a sixth grade teacher in Madison, helped me frame the story and read several chapters as it took shape. My son Steve, who is a staff photographer for the *Wisconsin State Journal* in Madison, read several drafts. Steve and I worked out a number of the scenes while we were canoeing in the Boundary Waters Canoe Area Wilderness. My youngest son Jeff, a Colorado businessman, made excellent suggestions for improving one of the later versions of the book. And my wife, Ruth, read page after rewritten page as the novel slowly took shape over many months.

As I researched this book, my twin brothers, Donald and Darrel, and I reminisced about the many hours we spent picking cucumbers when we were farm kids in Waushara County, Wisconsin. I thank them for the memories they recalled in vivid detail. Donald also worked for the Chicago Cucumber Company, at their receiving station in Wild Rose, Wisconsin, and a good friend, Jim Kolka, worked for the Libby, McNeil and Libby cucumber receiving station in Wild Rose, during the time I worked for the H. J. Heinz Company. Don and Jim helped me remember those "pickle days" and the details of handling tons of cucumbers every day, seven days a week. I also gained some excellent information from Phillip Gohlke, a longtime cucumber grower from the Nesh-koro area. Phil helped me recall some of the details of these old cucumber salting stations, the setting for this story.

I extend a special thanks to Kate Thompson, who spent several hours with the manuscript, straightened out the timeline, and helped me sharpen many of the scenes in the book. Mary Lou San-tovec, formerly of Badger Books, read the manuscript and caught many errors. Marshall Cook, LaMoine MacLaughlin, and Maryo Gard Ewell offered excellent suggestions for improving the story.

My heartfelt thanks to those who continue to read my books and tell me they like them. These comments keep me writing.

And finally, I dedicate this book to my daughter, Sue.

In a Pickle

1

Pickle Patch

Andy Meyer watched the pickup's progress from the cucumber patch just south of the farmstead where he was hoeing. He took off his straw hat and rubbed his sleeve across his forehead—sweat trickling into his eyes had become a constant annoyance. He hadn't seen the pickup before. He knew all the neighbors' vehicles—their cars, trucks, and tractors—and this looked too new and too shiny for their rural community.

A dust cloud swirled up from the country road as the truck sped past Stewart's place and continued north. A fine dusting of talcum-like dirt accumulated on the hazel brush and the lower leaves of the oak trees that grew on both sides of the road. It covered the dry grass that crowded the road, spread out into the ditches, and floated over a cow pasture where a dozen or so Holsteins paused in their grazing. The day was hot and humid so the dust hung suspended for a time before settling—a dirty brown cloud that country people were accustomed to seeing during the dry days of summer.

The shiny green 1955 Chevrolet turned into the Meyer farmstead, almost missing the driveway because the driver was going too fast. The cloud of dust rolled on down the road before it thinned and disappeared.

Andy wondered who the visitor was—few vehicles traveled this remote stretch of country road. Jens Swanson, the mail carrier, had appeared at ten-thirty this morning, as he did every morning except Sunday. The milkman, Wilbur Witt, came shortly after eight each day to pick up the Meyers' five cans of milk, the product from the morning and previous evening's milkings. The milk had been cooling in a water tank in the pump house, where well water flowed around the cans on its way to the stock tank in the barnyard. By now, mid-afternoon, the Meyer milk, along with milk from the other farmers in the community, was already being made into cheese at the Link Lake Cheese Factory.

The pickup truck was unexpected, a stranger in the community. An unknown vehicle stopped work momentarily, turned heads, and raised questions.

Andy kept his deep blue eyes on the truck as it traveled up the Meyers' driveway. Tall and slim, Andy wore faded blue overalls, a blue chambray shirt, and a straw hat. He had brown hair, and his face and arms were deeply tanned from hours spent working outside. His big, calloused hands held the hickory hoe handle, which he now leaned on as he watched the pickup's progress.

Andy limped slightly, a reminder of the wound he had received in the Korean War, four years earlier. He had been drafted only a few months after graduating from Link Lake High School in 1950 and had ended up a platoon sergeant. He was shot during the battle of Bloody Ridge in September of 1951. Afterward, he had spent four months in a hospital recovering from his wounds, with but two thoughts filling his mind—his girlfriend, Amy Stewart, and the home farm, which he planned to take over from his dad.

While he was in the service, Andy's buddies told him how they looked forward to jobs in the big cities, working in factories, working eight-to-five jobs. Andy shared his dreams of living on a small farm where he was close to nature and the land, where the work was hard and the days long. His army friends didn't know what to make of this young man from Wisconsin, whose dreams seemed so small compared to those contemplating the bright lights of the city. But Andy always had a smile and was a friend to nearly everyone he met, no matter if their dreams were different from his.

If Andy worked hard, in one day he could hoe all the rows of his family's half-acre cucumber patch, located on a little rise next to the white pine windbreak and just south of the red barn. Just about every farmer in this part of Ames County, Wisconsin, had a cucumber patch, called a pickle patch. They planted cucumbers as a cash crop—a way to make money faster than milking cows or raising pigs. Most of the cucumber patches were only a half acre or so, because their cultivation, from planting the seeds to hoeing and picking, required hand labor. Picking cucumbers, the worst of the tasks, required bending over and snapping the spiny cucumbers from their scratchy vines and tossing them into a five-gallon pail, one cucumber at a time. Now and again a family with several kids would plant an acre or more. In fact, you could tell how many kids a farmer had merely by looking at the size of his cucumber patch. Of course, most city people passing through couldn't tell the difference between cucumber, green bean, and potato plants, especially when they were little, at the cultivating and hoeing stage.

Andy's pa, Isaac Meyer, now in his sixties, worked at the other end of the patch. He drove a big Percheron draft horse, a roan gelding named Claude, between the rows of cucumber plants. Claude was hitched to a one-row cultivator that turned the brown sandy soil and buried a scattering of ragweed and pigweed that had managed to escape earlier cultivations. Isaac also saw the dust and the pickup speeding down their gravel road, but he kept going, kept the big roan walking between the rows while he held the handles of the cultivator.

Isaac, as tall and thin as a cedar fence post, was mostly bald with a fringe of gray hair circling his head above his ears. Daily outside work had deeply tanned the lower part of his face; his bald head remained chalky white because he always wore a hat. His penetrating gray eyes, peering through steel-rimmed glasses, now stayed focused on the row ahead.

The cultivator uprooted the weeds between the cucumber rows, but hoeing, a slow, tedious, but necessary job, was the only way to remove weeds within the rows. Andy didn't mind hoeing, because you could quickly see what you'd accomplished. No waiting for results.

The pickup stopped near the farmhouse. Buster, the Meyers' big collie, announced the stranger's arrival with a few loud barks and then watered one of the truck's hind tires. A man in a gray felt hat and suspenders climbed down out of the truck, ignoring Buster, and walked up to Andy's ma, who was hanging clothes on the line, a series of wires strung between posts in back of the big white farmhouse and near the "two-holer" outdoor toilet that stood fifty or so yards away, tucked up against a twenty-acre woodlot to the north. Mary was a short woman of ample proportions, with gray hair and sparkling blue eyes. She wore a flowered apron she had made from a flour sack. The apron came up just below her chin and tied in the back. Andy could see his ma smiling as the stranger approached her.

As Andy's ma and the stranger talked, Buster smelled his trousers, but the man continued to ignore the dog. He jumped back when Buster jammed his nose into his crotch, as the dog was prone to do, whether the visitor was man or woman.

Looks like another feed salesman, Andy thought. Seemed every week or so another one stopped at their farm, trying to sell some new mineral mixture for the cattle, or a feed supplement "guaranteed to put a few more pounds of milk in every milk pail," or a new fertilizer that would "put more oats in the bin and more corn in the crib." Andy and his dad tired of these interruptions. These salesmen, although their products differed, all used the same approach. They argued smoothly—too smoothly for Andy—that to succeed as a farmer, you must push your cows to milk more, fertilize your soil to produce more. More is better. Andy simply didn't agree with this approach. His grandfather and his father had done reasonably well without constantly expanding their operations, and he planned to farm the same way—without trying to do more all the time. Yet, Andy always was friendly toward these men, as was his nature.

Ma was pointing to the cucumber patch, and soon the fellow headed on foot up the hill in back of the barn. Andy continuing hoeing, not looking forward to the interruption. The man walked between two rows of cucumbers, raising little puffs of dust as he moved along. He had a pipe in his mouth.

A few yards away, he called out, "You Andy Meyer?" His voice sounded like he had gravel in his mouth. He talked out of the side of his face, like part of it didn't work.

"I am," Andy replied. He pushed back his straw hat and once more leaned on his hoe handle.

"Well, you're the fellow I'm lookin' for. Damn, it's hot out here. Sun's a scorcher."

"That it is," Andy said. "Good day for growing corn and cukes." He was waiting for the sales spiel.

"You the manager of the Harlow pickle factory in town?"

"I am."

"Well, I'm your boss. Name is J. W. Johnson." Andy put out his hand for a handshake. Johnson did not extend his hand. "I'm district manager for the H. H. Harlow Pickle Company."

There was a moment of silence. A slight breeze blew out of the west, rustling the needles in the white pine windbreak. The smell of pine drifted across the pickle patch, mixing with the smells of freshly disturbed soil.

"Glad to meet you," Andy said. But he was not sure he meant it.

This Johnson fellow seemed mighty different from his previous boss, who had hired Andy to manage the Harlow pickle factory in Link Lake during the summer cucumber harvest season in 1952, right after Andy had come home from the army. He had been surprised at the offer because he had not worked at the pickle factory previously, but he gladly accepted. Andy and his previous boss, a fellow named Smitt, had hit it off the first time they met, and Smitt had said, "The job of running the pickle factory is yours."

The H. H. Harlow Pickle Company, headquartered in Chicago, built the Link Lake Pickle Factory in the 1930s, during the depths of the Great Depression, when farmers in central Wisconsin and all across the nation were struggling to save their land from bankruptcy and attempting to earn enough money to keep their families fed and clothed. Cucumbers became a ready source of income, more dependable in some ways than potatoes, which had been a cash crop since wheat growing died out in central Wisconsin and farmers shifted to dairy cows. Farmers who grew potatoes worked hard and gambled they'd make a dollar or two. A farmer could not predict what the price would be when he sold the crop in late winter. From harvest time to selling time he had to store the potatoes and keep them from freezing, which usually meant keeping a woodstove burning night and day in a potato cellar for several months.

Cucumbers were different. You picked cucumbers, hauled them to the pickle factory—where they were weighed and sorted by size—and you got your money right there on the spot. No waiting. Most farm products required a wait before the money came in. Even selling milk required a two-week wait for a milk check. But not cucumbers. During those long, dreadful, and often fearful Depression years, thousands of farmers in central Wisconsin had turned to growing cucumbers.

The Link Lake Pickle Factory operated from about mid-July to mid-September and the rest of the year stood vacant. Work at the factory consisted of taking in, sorting, grading, and weighing cucumbers; writing out checks to the farmers; and then dumping the cucumbers into huge vats with water and salt and allowing them to cure through the fall and early winter. In February, Harlow sent a crew to the pickle factory, and they emptied the vats and shipped the fermented cucumbers to a big Harlow plant in Chicago, where they were processed into dill pickles, slicers, sweet pickles, pickle spears, chips, relish, and the like.

In the 1940s, the Harlow pickle factory in Link Lake not only bought cucumbers and salted them in storage vats, it also packed cucumbers in fifty-gallon wooden barrels along with dill, salt, and the other ingredients to make dill pickles. Dill pickle barrels were lined up in back of the factory by mid-August. The dill pickle maker—one man with that sole responsibility—packed fresh cucumbers into the barrels, added the dill weed and salt, set the wooden covers in place, filled the barrels with water, pounded the bunghole plugs home, and moved the barrels down a little wooden track constructed for that purpose. The dill pickle-making process also required that the pickle maker roll the barrels each day, to make sure the ingredients were mixing with the fresh cucumbers.

Andy's pa reached the end of a row. He turned Claude, and they slowly moved toward Andy and Johnson.

"This'll be your fourth year managing our factory in Link Lake."

"Yes, it will."

"Gonna make some changes," Johnson growled. He looked up to see the horse and cultivator almost upon him. He stepped over a couple of rows so the cultivator could pass.

"Whoa," Isaac Meyer said. Claude stopped, dropping his head. The big horse was breathing hard, sweat streaking his reddish brown hide. He spread his hind legs, and a stream of urine hit the sandy ground, nearly splattering on Johnson.

"Chrissake," Johnson said, jumping out of the way. "Damn horse just about pissed on me."

The pungent smell of horse urine mixed with horse sweat, fresh turned soil, and white pine.

Isaac smiled. "Howdy," he said to Johnson.

"Got business with your kid, here," Johnson said. "I'm district manager for the Harlow Pickle Company."

"Oh," Isaac said, still smiling. "Giddap." The big gelding took up the slack in the tugs, and the cultivator once more began moving down the field, Isaac holding the handles with the horse reins around his shoulders.

"This all the cukes you got—this little bitty patch?" Johnson asked. He was scratching himself under his arm. "Can't be more than a half acre if it's that. No money in these little pickle patches. No money a-tall."

Andy had a response to J. W. Johnson's idea about cucumber patches, but he decided that sometimes it's best to keep your thoughts to yourself. That's what his pa always said. "There's a place to speak your mind. Trouble is lots of folks can't seem to figure out where that place is."

"Times are changin'. If you're gonna be in the cucumber business, then you've gotta have cucumbers, not just the few sacks that you pick off a little patch like this. Got to have acres of cucumbers. Cucumber fields, not pickle patches." Johnson was waving his arms in a big sweep.

Andy thought about all the Christmas presents these little patches had bought, all the school clothes and books and BB guns, .22 rifles, and bikes. Still, he said nothing.

Andy and Johnson talked for a few more minutes about possible dates the pickle factory might open and whether Andy had his help lined up to start once the cucumbers began pouring in. Abruptly, Johnson said, "Just too damn hot out here for talkin' or just about anything else. Don't know how you poor bastards stand it—you dirt farmers who keep doin' things the old-fashioned way. All this is gonna change soon. Gonna change. Mark my words."

With that, Mr. J. W. Johnson, district manager for the H. H. Harlow Pickle Company, strode off toward his new green pickup. He was thinking about how to replace Andy Meyer as pickle station manager, but it was too late for this season. He knew he'd have somebody different in that spot next year. Now his mind was on a glass of Point Special Beer, on tap at his favorite tavern, the Deer Horn Bar, in nearby Willow River, where he had a small office on Main Street. Besides that, the tavern was air-conditioned.

Buster had watered each of the four tires of the pickup. Andy's ma continued to hang up clothes. She looked toward Johnson and smiled, but he didn't so much as wave as he climbed back into the dusty truck. He gunned the engine and sent gravel stones flying as he roared down the driveway and turned south, once more sending up a great cloud of yellow dust that hung over the road before slowly drifting east.

Andy and his dad rested near one of the big pine trees in the shade, the big gelding standing nearby.

"Whatta you make of Mr. J. W. Johnson?" Andy asked as he took off his straw hat and wiped his forehead with a big red handkerchief.

"A pompous ass," Isaac said. The words hung in the muggy air.

"Gonna be a long pickle season, working with Johnson," Andy said. "If he blew himself up any bigger, he'd bust." He smiled when he said it.

"Expect he would. Expect he would," Isaac said.

"Have to learn how to work with him," Andy muttered. "Not gonna be any fun." He turned back to his hoeing.

2

Birthday Party

Isaac Meyer would be sixty-five on June 18. Some of the neighbors said they should throw a party for him at the country school. Isaac wasn't much for parties—wasn't much for having anybody call attention to him. He preferred to be at home on his 160 acres, which his grandfather had homesteaded back in 1867 after spending some time fighting in the Civil War. Isaac's wasn't the best farm that God ever made. The land was sandy and as a result mighty droughty. Crops did best if it rained every week, and anybody who knows anything about farming knows that the rains seldom come when they're supposed to, or at least when a farmer hopes they'd come. Too many summers the rains didn't come on time, or the clouds didn't drop much water, and the crops in the Rose Hill School District, including Isaac's, didn't amount to much if they amounted to anything at all.

After considerable discussion across the Meyer kitchen table—with Mary leading the talk and with substantial support from Andy—Isaac gave in and said a party would be all right, but he didn't want any gifts. They set it for a Saturday night, the day of his birthday, at the Rose Hill schoolhouse.

Birthday Party

The Rose Hill schoolhouse was a tired old building, built in the 1890s and now showing its age. It stood perched on a hill with a decent view in three directions, especially to the east, where you could catch a reasonable look at the waters of Link Lake in the distance. Once painted a brilliant white, the school was now faded and gray. Putty around its big windows on the north and south had mostly fallen away, and during the cold days of winter, frigid air seeped into the building everywhere, challenging the big wood-burning stove that stood alone in the back of the room.

The Rose Hill School teaches first through eighth graders, about twenty students each year, and all in one room. About the only use for the school during the hot summer months was the occasional anniversary celebration or birthday party, and infrequent school board and school district meetings.

With the children off on summer vacation, the acre schoolyard had grown up to grass and weeds. Tall grass grew over the wooden teeter-totter. The softball diamond, with home plate just in front of the boy's outhouse, was scarcely visible, except for the sandy place where the batter stood, and the little grass-free area for the pitcher. Grass, ragweed, and even a Canada thistle or two had grown up around the once-red woodshed. One end of the building sheltered the pump, where a pump jack powered by an electric motor jerked the pump rods up and down, spewing a little stream of water into the pail that older kids toted into the schoolhouse.

As the day of his party neared, Isaac fussed about what to wear and whether he'd be asked to say anything to the crowd, a task he dreaded more than cleaning manure out of the hen house on a hot day. Mary told him the whole thing would be painless, and if he set his mind to it, he might even have a good time.

Birthday Party

"Going to my own birthday party ain't my idea of havin' a good time," Isaac said. "It's one thing to be gettin' on in years, but it's quite another wastin' time celebratin' the fact."

"It'll go fine," Mary said, smiling. She knew her husband well. They'd been married back in 1920, and Andy hadn't come along until 1930, a bit of a surprise for both of them, but a welcome one, as Andy had turned out just fine. He'd even said he wanted to stay on the home place and keep on farming their quarter section after they couldn't manage anymore. That's about the best thing a farmer could hear from a son.

Mary suggested that they drive their rusty 1950 Ford pickup over to the school so that Andy could have the car to pick up Amy Stewart. Andy and Amy had known each other since they attended Rose Hill School together. Although they'd been friends all through elementary school, the two really hadn't taken a special liking to each other until Andy was a senior in high school and Amy was a sophomore and Andy asked her to the senior prom. At first Amy thought it might be similar to dancing with your brother, but after that night at the prom she knew there was something special between them, and it wasn't like being brothers and sisters. When Andy was fighting in Korea, she wrote to him everyday, trying to cheer him up and keeping him apprised of happenings at home.

Amy, Jake and Emma Stewart's only child, had grown up doing boy's work around the farm: driving tractor, helping milk cows, making hay, doing all the things expected of farm kids. For years she had been a gangly, long-legged kid, not homely, but not much to look at either. But when she started high school and began filling out she became, at least in Andy's mind, the best-looking girl at Link Lake High. She had long, blonde hair that shone when the sun hit it just right and blue eyes that matched the waters of Link Lake. Her smile, well, when Amy Stewart smiled a dreary place lit up and became cheerful.

Amy had studied typing and bookkeeping in high school, so it wasn't hard for her to find a good job. After she graduated she got a job in Racine with J. I. Case, the company that made Case tractors, combines, and other such farm equipment. Problem was, Racine was a considerable distance from Link Lake, and she came home only every month or so. She had made a special effort to come home for Isaac's birthday party because the Stewart and Meyer families had been friends for three generations, and she looked forward to some time with her boyfriend, Andy.

Amy had a notion that Andy wanted to marry her but was just too bashful to ask. If he did ask, she didn't know how she'd answer. She wasn't so sure she wanted to spend her life farming the way Andy and his dad did. She knew that if they got married Andy could immediately go to work for her father, on the Stewart home place—something Jake Stewart was hoping for because he had always liked Andy. But she first had to convince Andy that farming with an old Farmall tractor and horses, and milking only fifteen cows and planting a half acre of cucumbers each summer, like he did now, would never get them anyplace. After all, her father farmed a thousand acres, milked thirty-five cows, grew two-hundred acres of corn, planted thirty acres of cucumbers and a hundred acres of potatoes, and had regular visits from the county agricultural agent, who kept him up to date on new agricultural research.

By the time Isaac and Mary got to the school, the three-piece band—made up of Albert Olson strumming the banjo, Thomas

John Jones on the fiddle, and Louie Pixley fingering the concertina—had tuned up and was ready to go. They sat on chairs right in front of the old brown teacher's desk, which had been pushed up against the back wall, just under the blackboard that stretched all the way across the back of the school. Abraham Lincoln and George Washington stared down from above the blackboard, and just beneath them was a sample of script writing and formal lettering that students were supposed to practice when they finished their other homework.

Someone had pushed the school seats, scarred with the initials of generations of students, to the sides of the room, leaving a reasonable space for dancing in the middle. As Isaac and Mary came through the door, the band struck up its first tune, an old-fashioned polka that made your feet begin tapping whether you were a dancer or not.

"I hope you ain't expectin' me to dance?" Isaac whispered to his wife.

"Not unless you want to," she said.

"Can't recall the last time I polka danced."

"Maybe we should try it, see if we remember how."

"Later, maybe. Ain't as young as I used to be."

Card tables in the back of the room sagged with casseroles and sandwiches—bologna, cheese, and chicken salad—red Jell-O with bananas, baked beans, cold chicken, white cake, and chocolate cake with cherries. A big birthday cake adorned with six big candles and five little ones stood in the middle of one of the tables. Nobody wanted to stick sixty-five candles on a cake.

When Andy and Amy arrived a few minutes later, they immediately began dancing. The band had shifted to an old-time waltz, the kind where you can swing around the floor but still do a little snuggling with your partner if snuggling is what you have on your mind.

Isaac was greeting his neighbors, John Korleski, who lived just across the field to the east; Allan Clayton, who lived to the north; Floyd Jenks, whose land bordered his on the west; and of course Jake Stewart, who farmed a vast acreage to the south. Isaac and Jake had grown up together, gone to school together, and played softball together, but now they seemed to have drifted apart, since Jake had taken up "big-time farming" as Isaac called it.

But on this night differences were set aside as the neighbors of the Rose Hill School District celebrated Isaac's sixty-fifth birthday. Talk about closing the school was on the minds of some people, and attending Isaac's party reminded them of how important this little school building had been to them and their families. The school had operated for seventy-five years.

Jake Stewart was one of the chief supporters of closing down the place. Because he was president of the Rose Hill school board, and because he had so many acres of farmland and hired a fair number of people to work for him, his word had considerable clout. Jake had one ear out for the Department of Public Instruction people in Madison, who constantly pushed him to convince his neighbors that closing the school was a good idea. The university in Madison occasionally sent up some young researchers to hammer the nail with talk about better math scores, better reading scores, better nearly everything if the kids out here were bused to the Link Lake Consolidated School.

People listened to Jake because it was kind of comical to hear him talk, even though his ideas were generally not what many of his neighbors believed in or wanted to hear. Jake was a tall, skinny fellow with thick gray hair and a chin nearly as wide as his fore-head. He walked like he was headed into a strong wind, always leaning forward, to the extent that some folks predicted that one day he'd just topple over face first and drive that big chin of his straight into the ground. He talked with a kind of high-pitched twang. If you weren't looking at him when you were hearing him, you'd swear it was a woman talking—lots of folks said that, but not to Jake's face, of course.

Thoughts about the school's future swirled through people's minds as they danced the polka and old-time waltz, and even danced to songs from the old country, folk songs you'd call them. Haunting tunes, some of them, quiet and thoughtful and packed with meaning. Louie Pixley led these old tunes on his button concertina, which he could really make talk.

Andy and Amy stole away from the crowd and sat out on the front porch of the school, where they looked off toward Link Lake in the distance. With a full moon, it was nearly as light as a cloudy day as they sat holding hands and watching the lights of Link Lake's Main Street, not much brighter than fireflies at this distance. The lake itself was a black emptiness surrounded by trees and fields.

"You still like your job?" Andy asked.

"It's okay. Pay is good," Amy answered.

Andy could see the moonlight on her hair. He squeezed her hand a little and then put his arm around her, pulling her close. She put her head on his shoulder.

"We had good times at this school," Amy said.

"I remember how you hit a softball farther than about anyone."

"Did a lot of farm chores in those days."

"Remember the dirty trick that you and Kate Hampton played on Claude Olson and me when we were in high school?"

"Sure do," Amy said, smiling. "That'll teach you to go skinny-dipping in Link Lake."

"How'd you and Kate find out we were out there that night?"

"That's my little secret."

"Wasn't a very nice thing you girls did, running off with our clothes. And then just sitting there on shore and waiting for us to get cold enough so we'd have to come out of the lake bare naked."

"You and Claude were a sight to see, backing out of the water and covering up with both hands what you didn't want us to see." Amy was giggling softly, as only she could.

"It was mighty embarrassing. About as embarrassing as it can get."

"Don't think I ever told you how white your little behind was, compared to your tan back. Just as white as fresh snow."

"I don't want to hear any more about me being naked."

"It was very funny at the time. When I see Kate we still talk about it. Course she and Claude are married now. She must have seen something that appealed to her."

"Cut it out. You got me blushing right here in the dark."

Someone had begun singing Happy Birthday, and Amy and Andy walked back in the school to join in. A pause followed the singing. People expected Isaac to stand up and say a few words about what it was like being sixty-five years old. Finally he got to his feet.

"Well . . . well . . . well, I'm now sixty-five," he said. "Thanks . . . thanks for comin' to my party. Appreciate it." Then he paused as if to think of something else, and finally said. "Ah, hell," and sat down.

Birthday Party

Everybody clapped and came by to shake his hand and tell him what a good neighbor he had been all these years and wish him lots more years of good health.

The full moon washed the countryside white as people filed out of the schoolhouse, got into their cars, and headed home. Isaac and Mary were among the last to leave.

"'Twas a good party," Isaac said as he fired up the old pickup and headed back home, along the dusty country road.

3

Pickle Factory

"Gonna be a good pickle year," Isaac Meyer said at the breakfast table one morning a few weeks after his birthday party. "Be pickin' cukes in a few days. Blossoms all over the place and a few little pickles peekin' out here and there. Yup, gonna be a good pickle year. Maybe make a little extra money for a change."

Of course the weather was a big factor in cucumber growing, and scarcely a week went by that the *Link Lake Gazette* didn't include an article about the weather—too much rain, not enough rain, temperatures too cool, temperatures too hot. Growing season early. Growing season late. Nothing was ever just right with the weather. But this year, especially in May and June, the rains were timely and the temperatures warm. It was just the kind of early summer weather a farmer wants to give crops a good start before the inevitable dry weather of late summer sneaks into the area, quietly and without notice, and slows everything down— sometimes killing the crops if it hangs on too long.

The corn had grown to knee high by the Fourth of July, and now, a week later, the oats stood tall and ripening, the cow pastures remained green and growing, the potatoes stood yardstick tall, and the cucumber patches had come on better than most years.

"Be openin' that pickle factory soon, Andy?" Isaac asked.

"Expect so," Andy said. "Got a lot of cleaning up before we can start taking in cukes. Place is always dusty and dirty after sitting idle all winter. Waiting for this guy Johnson to call, to say when I should get started."

Andy had no more than said the words when the phone rang, and his mother got up to answer. "It's Mr. Johnson," she whispered.

"Hello," Andy said into the mouthpiece of the old wall phone. He held the black receiver to his ear.

"This here is J. W. Johnson. You got that pickle factory in Link Lake ready to go?" Andy would know the gravely voice anywhere.

"No," Andy answered. "I was waiting for your call."

"Well, I'm calling, and you'd better get on down there 'cause the place is a mess. Stopped in last week for a look around."

"It's always a mess after a long winter," Andy started to explain.

"I'll meet you there tomorrow morning at eight," Johnson interrupted. "Don't be late. I don't put up with nobody being late," he growled.

"I'll be there," Andy said. As he hung up, he thought, *Who does he think he is, telling me to be on time? What am I? Some lowly worker who doesn't know enough to crawl out of bed in the morning? If he knew the first thing about farm people he wouldn't say anything about me being on time.*

Andy had already lined up the summer work crew, some folks who had worked other years and a few new ones, too. He had asked around who might be interested in working at the pickle factory and got a few suggestions. It was hard to find good help because most workers were busy in the summer. He had told them they'd be getting a buck an hour this year, up from seventy-five cents because President Eisenhower was expected to sign into law a new minimum wage of a dollar an hour. Andy and Helen Swanson, the bookkeeper, would receive $1.25 an hour.

Andy knew his crew was waiting to hear from him. First he called Blackie Antonelli. Blackie, whose real first name was Tony, lived near Redgranite. This would be Blackie's third year at the factory. His grandfather had come from Italy to work in the granite quarries, but the quarries had closed many years ago and the Antonellis, along with many other Italian immigrants, had found other work in the area. Blackie was twenty-one, five-and-a-half-feet tall, and as strong as a young bull. His black hair hung nearly to his shoulders—one of his defiant characteristics. His dark eyes bore right through you, especially when he was provoked. It didn't take much to provoke Blackie, either—a wrong word said and he was ready with his fists. He had a short fuse—but he liked Andy, and they got along well.

Andy asked Blackie if he could start work at eight the next morning to help with cleanup. Blackie said he'd be there.

Next, Andy rang up Paul "Quarter Mile" Sweet, who lived on a nearby farm. Folks in the neighborhood said Paul, though an excellent student, had a long way to go and was maybe only a quarter mile there. He was eighteen, the oldest of the four Sweet kids, and headed for college in Madison. He really needed the money. Neither his mother nor father had graduated from high school. He would be the first kid from his family to attend college.

Quarter Mile was nearly six feet tall, blond, wiry, and strong. He had sleepy blue eyes, and he smiled easily. This would be his first year at the factory. Andy thought helping with the cleanup would be a good way for Quarter Mile to get acquainted with the place and all its nooks and crannies. He asked the young man to come in at eight the next day.

He phoned the rest of the crew and asked them to come in on Tuesday. Helen Swanson, who kept the books and figured the salt for the pickle vats, was in her thirties. Like Andy, this would be her fourth year at the pickle factory. She worked as secretary for the Link Lake High School during the school year, and Andy had heard she was recently divorced.

Arthur "Preacher" Ketchum was new to the crew this year. He ministered to a small flock of believers that crowded into the Church of the Holy Redeemed every Sunday morning. They heard him go on about how they were all headed straight to hell unless they followed the church's rules: "Don't watch movies— they are the devil's creation. Don't dance—it stirs up carnal thoughts. Stay out of the saloons—only the dregs of the earth frequent them."

Preacher, in his mid-thirties, was thin, almost frail, and he didn't seem strong enough for the work. But he had come to Andy with a story about how poor his family was—he had a wife and four kids—and how they really needed the extra money, so Andy hired him. Of course they agreed that Preacher wouldn't have to work at the factory on Sundays, even though it was open.

At sixty, Agnes Swarsinski was the oldest person on the crew— and in some ways the youngest. This would be Agnes's fifth year at the pickle factory, and she was the life of the party. She could make people laugh when there was absolutely nothing to laugh about. Agnes was the second generation of Polish people who had immigrated to northern Ames County directly from Poland. They were farm folks who worked hard, managed to eke out a living on their small, sandy, and often stony farms, and believed in helping their neighbors.

Agnes looked worn. Her face was wrinkled, her big hands calloused from years of farm work, and she wore her mostly gray hair tied with a little ribbon at the back of her head. But Agnes's eyes caught your attention. It wasn't their color so much as the way they sparkled, especially when she was telling a story or giving you a little of her rural wisdom. Her family spoke Polish at home, and she had a definite accent. She greeted everyone with, "Hey der, honey," and a smile that took up much of her wrinkled face. She forever poked fun at her own nationality. For instance, one day last year she had asked, "What makes a Polack's eyes light up? You don't know? Well, you stick a flashlight in his ear."

The next morning Andy borrowed his pa's Ford pickup and drove the four miles from their farm to the factory at the west edge of Link Lake. He got there about seven-thirty so he'd have some time before J. W. Johnson arrived to see how the building had made it through the winter and what repairs looked necessary. The pickle factory, a low-slung building about sixty feet long and half that wide, stood in a little hollow against a spur line for the Chicago and Northwestern Railroad, which separated the factory from the Link Lake Sawmill. The factory was built in the 1930s and had been painted a dark green, but now the building had faded and was moving toward a dull nondescript gray.

Andy walked up the outside stairs to the main floor, fished in his pocket for the key to the big brass padlock, unlocked it, and pulled the door open. The hinges on the door squeaked, as they had every summer he had worked there. With all the effort to keep the cucumber sorters and other equipment working, he never remembered to squirt a little oil on the hinges.

Pickle Factory

Andy slid open the two big doors, revealing the unloading area and filling the space with sunlight. The pickle factory consisted of one large, open room, with bare wood walls. The only other source of light was a half-dozen bare bulbs hanging here and there from the bare board ceiling. A few feet back from the unloading area stood the cucumber sorter—twelve feet long, three feet wide, and four feet tall. The machine sorted the cucumbers into five size grades; farmers were paid accordingly, with the smallest cucumbers commanding the highest price. Constructed of wood and painted green, the sorter had sprockets and link chains running this way and that. An electric motor powered the sorter, which moved the cucumbers along its length with a shaking action. The slats on which the cucumbers moved were closer together in the front of the sorter, and farther apart at the back. Thus the smaller cucumbers fell between the slats first and tumbled into boxes where they were collected and weighed, followed by increasingly larger cucumbers until the largest, the number-five cucumbers, tumbled over the back of the sorter where they fell into boxes.

Inside the building were a dozen pickle vats, which looked like little silos, each about eight feet high and eight to fourteen feet across. The vats were made of redwood, the same material used for many farm silos. Each was encircled with half-inch metal rods that kept the wooden staves together, spaced two feet apart. The building was constructed around the vats, which rested on the ground. The main floor of the factory was five feet above the ground, so when you stood on the floor, only about three feet of the vats showed.

Square, wooden bushel-size crates constructed of wooden slats an inch apart were stacked from floor to ceiling along the south wall of the building. Each had the words "H. H. Harlow" emblazoned on a slat near the top.

The tracks of the Chicago and Northwestern line ran along the west side of the building. The salt bin was located in the northwest corner of the factory's large main room. This enclosed area, which started at ground level with a concrete floor and went almost to the ceiling of the building, had reinforced walls six inches thick to keep the tons of salt dry and to keep it from breaking the walls and gushing out into the building.

At the northeast corner of the building, boarded off from the rest, stood a little office, with unpainted board walls and a rustic desk with an old wooden kitchen chair pushed up next to it. A bookshelf above the desk held several Harlow guidebooks—everything from photos of diseased cucumbers to how to figure salt for the brine vats. A 1954 girlie calendar hung on the wall. One of last year's workers had hung it up, and Andy had left it there.

"Anybody here?"

"Yeah, by the salt bin," Andy answered.

"This damn place is a disaster," Johnson said as he looked around. "Looks worse than it did the other day when I was here."

"It's been just sitting here since last September," Andy said.

"Never saw one of our pickle factories so damn dirty."

"Got a couple of my men coming in later this morning."

"Good," said Johnson. This was the first time he'd told Andy he'd done anything right.

Johnson began unrolling posters and stapling them to the factory walls. One was a large painting of a white-haired woman with a jar of cucumbers on her kitchen table. A wood-burning cookstove stood behind her. "Mother Harlow's Country Made Pickles," the large print read. Andy smiled because he knew that none of Harlow's pickles had ever seen the inside of a farm kitchen, especially one with a wood-burning stove.

Johnson tacked up another sign, this one featuring a cucumber field with rows extending as far as a person could see. "Bringing Nature's Bounty to Your Table," the inscription read. Large print across the top of the poster shouted, "H. H. Harlow Pickle Company, Chicago, Illinois."

Signs reading "Quality Comes First," and "Mother Harlow Knows Best" followed. Andy didn't say anything; the signs added a bit of color to the brown walls.

His posters hung, Johnson moved on to inspect the office. A few minutes later, Blackie Antonelli and Quarter Mile Sweet arrived, and Andy introduced them to Johnson, who growled a greeting.

"Damndest mess I ever saw," he said. "Get that naked woman off the wall," he ordered. He was pointing at the girlie calendar. "This here is a business place, not some kind of peep show."

Andy didn't take the time to respond. He showed Blackie and Quarter Mile where the brooms and cleaning supplies were stored and put them to work. Then he returned to the office, where Johnson was still fussing.

"Where're your salt records?" Johnson said as he pulled open the desk drawer and began fumbling through the papers.

"Your office has them," Andy answered. "I sent them in last fall."

"Oh," Johnson said. "Where're the payroll records?"

"You got those, too."

"Well, what the hell kind of records have you got?" Johnson fumed.

"Haven't got any. Sent them all in."

"Helluva way to manage a business," Johnson snarled. "Place is filthy, records are missing, and tomorrow you open."

He stormed out of the office and almost ran over Blackie, who was sweeping just outside the door.

"Kid, you need a haircut. Don't want no long-haired workers around here. Mother Harlow likes things neat and tidy."

Blackie didn't even look up.

"You hear me, kid? You git that long hair chopped off."

"Yeah," Blackie said. He wasn't one to take orders from strangers, no matter who they were.

"What'd you say, kid?"

"I said, 'yeah.'"

"Does that mean you're gettin' your hair cut?"

"I didn't say that," Blackie answered.

Andy could see Blackie bristling, growing madder by the second. One thing about Blackie—you never confronted him like Johnson was doing. When you did, you might end up with a busted nose, no matter who you were.

"Better clean up that corner back of the vats, Blackie," Andy said.

Blackie whirled around and stormed off to the back of the factory.

"Young wiseass," Johnson said. "You see he gets his hair cut, or he's out of work. You hear me?"

"I hear you," Andy said, but he had no mind to force Blackie Antonelli to cut his hair. As long as it didn't get in the machinery or hang over his eyes so he couldn't see, Andy didn't care how long Blackie's hair was.

"I'll be back with the records this afternoon," Johnson said, climbing down the steps. "Better have this place shipshape by then."

Soon his shiny green pickup was kicking up gravel as he roared away. Andy knew right then that this pickle season was going to be a long one. The way Johnson was fussing and fuming, Andy wondered if he'd keep his job through the week.

Late that afternoon Johnson hurried into the pickle factory clutching a pile of records. He dropped them on the desk and growled to Andy, "Here's what you need." He glanced around the now clean and tidy factory and said to no one in particular, "Son of a bitch, but they got her polished up real good." And once again, he roared off in his pickup.

4

First Cukes

The day after the cleanup, Andy Meyer and his crew waited for the arrival of the first cucumbers, which would signal the start of the pickle season. Johnson had told him that Jake Stewart's new migrant boss would be bringing in at least one truckload of cucumbers by late afternoon. But Andy wondered if any of the small growers had seen the signs he had posted at the Link Lake Mercantile, at the Grist Mill, and at the Link Lake Cooperative announcing that the Harlow pickle factory was open for the 1955 season and paying $20 per hundred pounds for number-one cucumbers (the smallest, called gherkins, up to an inch-and-a-half in length), $15 for number twos, $10 for number threes, $5 for number fours, and fifty cents for number fives (six inches long and sometimes as big around as a woman's wrist).

The small ones brought the most money, but it took many of them to make a pound, while one number-five cucumber could weigh close to a pound itself. Problem always was how close to pick the cucumbers. Pick everything in sight and it might take four days before there were any more to harvest. Leave the littlest ones and in three days they'd be about right for number twos, which is where most farmers figured the money was—even if Harlow always emphasized picking the smallest ones. And of course no matter how good a pickle picker, some cucumbers continued hiding under a big leaf, or off in a corner somewhere to grow into number fours or number fives.

Andy had asked Helen Swanson to come in by eight on Tuesday morning, to set up the office and put in order the books that Johnson had dropped off. The rest of the crew showed up right after noon. Andy had them do some cleaning they'd not gotten done on Monday, but mostly they waited for the first cucumbers to arrive.

Agnes was busy trying to acquaint herself with the new people, Preacher Ketchum and Quarter Mile Sweet.

"Hey der, honey, what kinda preacher did you say you are?" Agnes asked the pastor.

"I am the shepherd for the flock of the Church of the Holy Redeemed."

"Shepherd, you say. You got sheep over there at that Church of the Holy something?"

"It's Holy Redeemed, madam."

"Well, you may be Holy Redeemed, but I ain't no madam. Never was, never will be."

"So be it," Preacher said, astonished at her response.

"Didn't your church come from them holy rollers or was they holy jumpers that used to set up here in Link Lake with their summer tent show? Remember that when I was a kid. They'd drive into town, put up that big old ratty tent down there by the lake. The preacher'd work everbody up so as some of them folks would commence jumpin' and yellin' and even rollin' on the ground. Yup, my pa said some of them folks got so excited they rolled right out the tent and kept right on a-goin'. Preacher told them folks they was headed to hell, and most of them commence believin' it, too."

"Are you saved, madam?" Preacher Ketchum asked, interrupting Agnes's reminiscence.

"Saved, hell yes I've been saved. At least three or four times I been saved. 'Member once when we was out in a boat on Norwegian Lake fishin' for bullheads and the boat took to leakin' real bad. Pa, he said we should hang on just a little longer 'cause them bullheads was bitin' pretty good. You know those big yella belly ones with the big ugly flat heads?" She looked around the room as if to make a comparison to those who had gathered around her and the preacher.

"Madam, I mean saved by the Lord," Preacher interrupted. But either Agnes didn't hear or she chose to ignore the question as she continued her story.

"By the time we got that old leaky boat beached, it was about sunk. About to go under. And I weren't no swimmer either. That old boat a-sunk, I'd been down there swimmin' with them big bullheads. There was another time I 'member bein' saved. We was milkin' cows then, the mister and me. Lightning struck the barn, came in on the metal stanchions, knocked down a bunch of the cows. Killed one and knocked me ass over end—pardon my French. Lost my hearing out of that deal, but it all came back in a couple weeks. Talk about being saved, why I know about being saved."

The rest of the factory crew was taking all this in, smiling and giggling, because those who knew Agnes knew this was just her way of having a little fun. Andy didn't interrupt her. He knew she could work with just about anybody. Some she made comfortable

34

right off the bat with her palaver, others she made squirm. Preacher Ketchum found himself in that second category.

Before Preacher had a chance to open his mouth with some sort of rebuttal, an old-model Chevrolet car pulled up to the loading dock. Three kids and their old man piled out and began hoisting gunnysacks of cucumbers onto the receiving platform. Andy recognized Pat Patterson, who farmed out by Saxeville on a few sandy acres.

"You get the prize for bringing in the first cukes of the season," Andy said as the pickle factory crew took their places by the big green sorter. "How's the crop this year, Pat?"

"Fair to middlin'. Could be better. Could be worse," Patterson said. He was a big burly man with a two-day growth of red whiskers. His redheaded kids climbed up the steps to the receiving platform and watched their cucumbers being dumped onto the sorter and jiggling along the machine from one end to the other, the little cucumbers falling into the first bushel box, the biggest ones holding on to the end and going over the back into a box. Most of them tumbled into wooden bushel boxes under the number-two and number-three chutes.

"Good looking cucumbers," Andy said as he watched them get sorted. "Got a good color. No blemishes."

"We try to take care of 'em," Patterson said. "Project for the kids, you know. A little extra money for 'em."

Andy knew that the Patterson family was scarcely making it. In fact, he'd heard they had missed a payment on their land taxes, so he knew the cucumber money was going for more than extra money for the kids.

Andy weighed each box when the sorting was done, wrote some numbers on a sheet of paper, and carried it over to Helen in the office. A few minutes later she handed a check to Andy, which he in turn gave to Mr. Patterson.

"I thank you for your business," Andy said, smiling.

Patterson glanced down at the check. "Hopin' it'd be a little more."

"Next time you'll do better. Crop is just starting. We get a rain in the next few days and your next check'll be a lot bigger."

Patterson got back in his car, and the old Chevrolet sputtered up the factory driveway, kicking up a little cloud of dust. Red-headed kids waved out the car windows.

5

Grist Mill

The same day the pickle factory opened, several farmers gathered a half-mile away at the Link Lake Grist Mill. The mill, a substantial three-story building, stood next to the concrete dam that stopped up the stream that poured out of Link Lake and held back enough water to provide the mill with power. City folks passing through town often stopped to photograph the mill and the water spilling over the dam. They claimed it was one of the most restful scenes in the area and that one look at the tumbling water had a kind of quieting affect on people and made them sleep better at night. Out here the locals figured a day picking cucumbers, or making hay, or shocking grain would do as much for a good night's rest as about anything that someone might think of, including watching water pour over a dam.

Water powered the dam, turned the big millstones, and had enough energy left to generate electricity, which the miller sold to the Wisconsin Power and Light Company.

The mill's exterior had once been painted a bright red, but now had declined to something less than pink. A porch was strung across the front of the building, and it was here that farmers hoisted their gunnysacks of cob corn and oats from their pickups, or from the back seats and trunks of their cars if they couldn't afford pickups. Once they had the gunnysacks on the porch, they dragged them into the mill proper. Three or four farmers always stood around, waiting to unload, waiting for the grinding, or waiting to load the sweet-smelling and still warm ground meal—now mixed ground oats and cob corn that the farmers would feed to their cows.

The mill had once ground wheat into flour, but since farmers stopped growing wheat fifty years ago and shifted to milking cows, the mill switched to grinding cow feed. The miller, Ole Olson, was a big Norwegian fellow whose father had come from the old country and taken up milling. Olson sported a big handlebar mustache; you couldn't tell its color—in fact, you couldn't tell much about the color of anything concerning Ole, because he was white from head to toe, covered with grain dust. A city kid viewing him on Halloween night would surely think he had seen a ghost.

Ole howdied everybody who pulled up to the mill, asked them about their families, and inquired about their cows and their crops. He was that kind of friendly fellow who made coming to the grist mill, a nearly weekly event for most farmers, a newsy experience.

On this Tuesday morning, Isaac Meyer had just unloaded several sacks of cob corn and oats from his Ford pickup and was dragging them to the square holes in the mill floor. He untied a gunnysack full of cob corn and dumped it in one of the holes, then a sack of oats, and then another bag of corn. The corn rattled down the metal tube on its way to the millstones for grinding, a few stray kernels flying about.

Grist Mill

Ole Olson never talked about his chickens, but he had a small flock of White Rock roasters in a chicken house in back of the mill, just behind the little red brick building that housed the electrical generator. Everyone figured that Ole had never bought a pound of feed in his life but depended on farmers' spilled grain to keep his chickens fed. In the fall he sold the live chickens to whoever wanted a good roaster for their oven. Nobody complained about Ole's chicken project because they knew he didn't earn much money grinding farmers' cow feed and selling a little electricity to the power company.

Oscar Wilson, a skinny little man from east of Link Lake, was waiting to unload, and Thomas John Jones, the fiddler—most everyone called him T.J.—waited for Ole Olson to weigh his grist so he could settle up and load his ground feed.

"How's the old man today?" T.J. said to Isaac with a smile, for he was recalling Isaac's sixty-fifth birthday party at the school.

"Able to get around," Isaac answered. "Able to get around."

"How the cows doin'?" T.J. asked.

"Purty good. Purty darn good. Pasture's been fair so far. When the pasture's green and growin', the cows do good. Pasture dries up, milk production goes down."

"Pretty fair milk prices this summer," Oscar Wilson chimed in.

"Could be better," Isaac said.

"Yup," said T.J. "Sure could. Never been able to figure out who's makin' the money on our milk. We sure as hell ain't."

"See the pickle factory opened up this morning. Your kid still runnin' the place?" inquired Wilson.

"Yeah, he is. Every year it's hard to find good help. Can you believe the preacher from that Church of the Holy Redeemed signed on this year?" Isaac said.

"'Spect they'll be gettin' a little religion while they're saltin' cukes," Ole Olson laughed. He had been listening to the conversation as he weighed T.J.'s sacks of ground feed on the scale.

"'Pears that way," Isaac said. "By the way, T.J., how your cukes doin' this year? You usually grow an acre. How they doin'?"

"Lookin' good. Nice and green. Good vines. Lots of vines. Kids and I'll start pickin' tomorrow if it don't rain."

"How about you, Oscar? How your cukes doin'?"

"Could be better. Got too many weeds. Didn't get the hoein' done. Hoein' came right in the middle of makin' hay, and I decided to make hay first." He paused for a moment. "Heard that your neighbor out there by Rose Hill School has himself thirty acres of cukes and a field full of Mexicans pickin'. Did I hear right?"

"Yeah, don't know what's got into Jake. He's been playing footsie with the Harlow Company that's encouraged him to put in those big fields. Cucumber experts from the college in Madison came right out to his farm and told him how he ought to set things up. Jake says that's the future. He thinks that some day Harlow won't be takin' in cukes from us little guys. That they'll only deal with the big growers like Jake Stewart."

"The hell you say," scoffed T.J. "We've had little pickle patches every year as long as I can remember and a long time before that. Jake musta got it wrong somewhere."

"Nah, it's what he tole me. Old Jake's got a bunch of shortcomings, but I've never known lying to be one of 'em," said Isaac.

"I tell ya, things are going to hell in the rural areas," said T.J. "'Fore you know it all us little guys will be out of business—be doing what Emil Simpson is doing. Remember Emil's farm out west of town? Fairly decent farm it was, somehow he couldn't make a go of it, couldn't pay his taxes, I guess. What's Emil doin' now? Sweeping floors at the Link Lake High School, that's what he's doin'. Damn shame for a man to go from farming to sweeping floors for a living."

"It is a damn shame," Isaac agreed. "But what's a man to do? He's gotta feed his family, put clothes on the kids' backs and food in their bellies. Know what happened to his farm, who bought it?" Isaac asked.

"Nope, ain't heard," said T.J.

Ole Olson piped up with the answer, "Guy and his wife from Milwaukee bought it. That's who did. They're gonna retire here, rent the land out to old Jake Stewart."

"Things is really going to hell around here, that's for sure," T.J. offered, shaking his head. He was loading his sacks of ground grain into his rusty pickup.

6

Pickle Factory Crew

After sorting, boxing, and weighing the few sacks of cucumbers the Patterson family had delivered, the pickle factory crew waited for the first truckload of cucumbers from Jake Stewart's place. J. W. Johnson had called and said the truck was on its way and that he'd be at the factory when it arrived, "to make damn sure everything goes the way it's supposed to." Andy thought, *The arrogant bastard. I've been running this place for four years and he wants to tell me how to sort cucumbers.*

While they were waiting, Agnes, Blackie, and Quarter Mile Sweet pulled some pickle crates together and began playing cards.

"Quarter Mile—you don't know how to play poker, do ya?" Blackie asked. Blackie didn't appreciate newcomers at the factory, especially college kids. He thought anyone going to college was a sissy and looking for a way to get out of work.

"Yeah, I know how to play poker," Quarter Mile said.

"How about you, Preacher, you good for a game of poker?" Blackie asked.

"Cards are the devil's work," Preacher said smugly. "The devil's work."

"Suit yourself—may be the devil's work, but it's the people's fun," Blackie said, grinning. Preacher turned and walked toward the factory office without saying anything.

"All right, we start with a little five-card stud," Blackie said. "Throw a nickel in the pot to get us started." Blackie tossed a nickel on the burlap bag they'd spread across a wooden pickle crate.

"You in, Agnes?" Blackie asked. His tone of voice changed when he talked to Agnes. He knew better than to mess with her; he knew she'd put him in his place, as she had a few times before. He remembered the first summer he worked at the pickle factory. He had said something about why such an old woman was allowed to do man's work. You'd have thought he'd hit a stick against a wasp's nest. She bristled up, grabbed him by the shoulders, and looked him straight in his dark eyes. Her usual good humor completely vanished.

"Listen to me, you little bastard—I'll do my job, you do your job. And you keep your big mouth shut about what's woman's work and what's men's work. You understand?"

Blackie was so stunned by Agnes's reaction that all he could think to do was shake his head up and down. Since that first bit of personal communication between Agnes and Blackie, they had gotten along fine.

"Yeah, I'm in," Agnes said, tossing in a nickel. Quarter Mile followed with his nickel, and Blackie began dealing.

"Say," Agnes said, her eyes sparkling, "did you hear the one about the fella who walks into a restaurant and asks the cook how he prepares their chickens?"

Quarter Mile, a good straight man, said, "No, don't think I have."

"'Well,' the cook replies, 'we don't do nothin' special. We just tell 'em they're gonna die.'"

There were groans all around as Blackie continued dealing the cards.

Andy thought this would be a good time to check on the condition of the rest of the pickle vats. He wanted to make sure the iron rods holding the wooden tanks together were tight and not slipping, and that there weren't any broken boards on the vat covers. These cover boards were forever breaking because workers piled boxes on top of them.

Helen Swanson sat at her desk in the office. A big, new colorful poster was thumbtacked to the wall behind her: a picture of a farm kitchen with a white-haired woman working over a wood-stove, having just removed a jar of cucumbers from the canner on the stove. Big red words shouted: "Mother Harlow Knows Good Dill Pickles."

"May I come in?" Preacher asked.

"Sure, come on in," Helen motioned to the one wooden chair that sat alongside the old, badly scarred wooden desk.

"You . . . you're crying," Preacher blurted out.

"No, something in the air is bothering me."

"Anything you want to talk about?" Preacher asked quietly. Helen's blonde hair came nearly to her shoulders. Her usually bright blue eyes were red and swollen.

"No . . . no, I don't think so." Helen fumbled with some papers on the desk and put them in a neat pile. "Nobody understands."

News travels fast in a small town, and Preacher knew that Helen had recently gotten divorced. He'd heard her husband, Karl, had returned from the Korean War a changed man, mostly for the worse. Before he was drafted, Karl Swanson had been well thought of in Link Lake, a star on the high school basketball team, and then a dependable employee at the Link Lake Sawmill. He married Helen just a few months before he left for Korea, and when he came back two years later, he spent every night and weekend in the Link Lake Tap. The sawmill foreman fired him when he came to work drunk one morning, and after that they depended on Helen's salary from her job at the high school. When he was home, which wasn't all that often, Karl just sat staring silently out the window of their little house. He mostly ignored Helen, and when he did talk to her he barked like a dog would bark at a stranger. As much as she loved him, Helen couldn't take it any longer, so she had filed for divorce. They had signed the final papers only a few weeks before the pickle factory opened.

"I know about your divorce," Preacher said quietly. He handed Helen his handkerchief, which she used to dab her eyes.

"It's just awful," she said between quiet sobs. "Just awful. I waited two years for Karl to come home, never went out, never even went to a movie, and when he came home I didn't know him. He was a different man. Not the Karl who climbed on the train and went off to war. War is hard on people. Very hard. I feel so sorry for him."

"Feeling sorry for him doesn't help," Preacher said.

"Still do, though. I still do."

The sound of a car door slamming stopped all activity in the pickle factory.

"Looks like we got a visitor," Agnes said. She quickly put away the cards and nickels while Blackie and Quarter Mile took apart their makeshift poker table. Preacher joined the others in the main room.

Andy was working in the basement of the factory and had heard the car door slam.

"Hello, Mr. Johnson," he said as he walked out the basement door toward his boss.

"Just call me J.W.," the district manager said in an unusually friendly manner. "Just call me J.W. You ready for Jake's trucks when they come in? Should be here in a half hour or so." Johnson was puffing on his pipe, which was almost always in his mouth.

Andy didn't know what to make of J. W. Johnson. One minute he was growling at him; the next, he was all buddy-buddy and chatty. Andy had met a few people like this before, and he knew to be wary of them.

"Come on up and meet the rest of the crew," Andy said. Together they climbed the steps to the main floor of the pickle factory. "Folks, this is J. W. Johnson, the district manager for H. H. Harlow, and my boss. Let's see, yesterday you met Quarter Mile Sweet and Blackie Antonelli."

"Hi, boys," Johnson said. Blackie expected some comment about his long hair but didn't hear it.

"This is Pastor Arthur Ketchum," Andy said. "He's working part-time for us, which means every day but Sunday."

"Always pleased to meet a man of the cloth," Johnson said, shaking the preacher's hand.

"And this is Agnes Swarsinski; she's been around here longer than I have. Nobody can spot a bad cucumber faster than Agnes."

"Glad to meet you, Agnes," Johnson made a little bow as he took her hand. "Good to have somebody on the sorter who knows how to pick out the bad cukes."

Andy and Johnson walked across the floor to the little office, where Helen was busy at her desk, thumbing through the thick book of directions for salting cucumbers.

"Helen, meet J. W. Johnson, our district manager."

"How do you do, sir," Helen said. Her eyes were still a little red. She stood up to shake Johnson's hand.

"Hear you're a wizard at figuring salt," Johnson said.

"I do my best," she answered.

"H. H. Harlow needs pretty little gals like you to brighten up the place. Glad you're part of the team. But what's a pretty gal like you doing figuring salt? Shouldn't you be home baking cookies?"

Andy rolled his eyes and escorted Johnson out of the office.

"See you got in a few cukes already," Johnson said.

"Yup, Patterson family out east of town has a half acre."

"Kind of a bother, ain't it, fussing with such a little amount?"

"It's not a bother. Not a bother at all. Kind of like meeting all the people and their kids when they come by."

"All this is gonna change," J. W. Johnson said. "It's all gonna . . ."

A big red truck heavily loaded with sacks of cucumbers slowly moved down the drive toward the pickle factory, and Johnson did not finish his thought.

7

Isaac and Jake

After driving home from the grist mill and unloading the cow feed in the feed room in the barn, Isaac went in the house, and he and Mary ate dinner. Their noon meal was always their biggest. Isaac couldn't understand why city folks wanted to call the noon meal lunch; for him lunch was something you ate after you finished playing cards at a neighbor's house or in the middle of a Sunday afternoon when relatives came calling.

After dinner Isaac moved over the wooden rocking chair by the cook stove, which burned wood on one side and had four gas burners on the other. He picked up the *Milwaukee Sentinel,* something he did after both the noon and evening meals. By day's end he had read the paper quite thoroughly. During football season he especially enjoyed reading about the Green Bay Packers—a person had to keep track of the Packers or he'd be left out of a goodly part of the fall conversation at the grist mill, the cheese factory, the Link Lake Tap, or about anywhere else a bunch of farmers got together. Something about a small-town team up against the likes of New York and Baltimore and all those other big-city football teams caught his attention. Unfortunately, the 1954 Packers had stunk up the field with a 4-8 record—only the Baltimore Colts, with 3-9, were worse. "Coach Blackbourn's got to go," Isaac said aloud after reading an article previewing the 1955 season.

He also followed the Milwaukee Braves closely, and now he checked the baseball scores. The Braves' new heavy hitter, Henry Aaron, who had joined the club in 1954, was batting over .300, and their pitcher, Warren Spahn, was one shifty thrower.

Isaac read about their U.S. senator from Appleton, Joe McCarthy, who had his wings clipped by the Senate last year after he'd ranted about Communists being sprinkled throughout the government, Hollywood, and just about everywhere, to the point that Isaac wondered if half his neighbors might be Communists and just weren't telling anybody. The once-popular Wisconsin politician had become an embarrassment.

He looked at the car ads, especially the new Ford Thunderbird, and thought he should stop at Link Lake Motors and at least have a look at one of these sleek new vehicles. He knew he'd never own one, though, because $2,995 was a pile of money to spend on a car, especially when his milk fetched only $3.50 for a hundred pounds. His fourteen cows, in total, gave about 450 pounds of milk a day during the summer, less in winter, so his milk checks for an entire year came to only about $4,000, and that had to cover all of his expenses.

He read about a new theme park, "Disneyland," that had just opened out in California. Sounded like a bigger version of the carnival that came to the Ames County Fair.

Before Isaac got to the editorials, which he usually turned to last, his chin had dropped to his chest and his eyes closed. Accustomed to this every-noon occurrence, Mary took the crumpled paper from his lap and continued clearing the table.

In a half hour or so, Isaac's eyes snapped open. "Think I'll pick the cucumbers this afternoon," he said as he got up from the rocking chair. He pulled on his straw hat and headed outside.

He searched for an old five-gallon pail he'd tucked away in the pump house, tossed it and a few gunnysacks in the back of the pickup, and bounced up the rutted field road to the cucumber patch. He parked in the shade of the white pine windbreak and started picking in the first row.

He moved slowly down the row, trying to pick every cucumber that was at least an inch long. His picking style was to straddle the row, with the pail to the side. That way he could use both hands to move the vines and pull the spiny cucumbers loose. When he was a kid, he'd learned that when you had to do something over and over again—like milking cows by hand, hoeing, or picking potatoes or cucumbers—if you got into a rhythm the work became natural and easy. The better the rhythm, the easier the job. It was hard to explain to someone what a work rhythm was all about because it was more than making your hands and your legs and your head work together—that was part of it to be sure, but not all.

Developing a rhythm for what some people might call boring work took the boring part out of it and elevated it to something that was hard to describe, but you knew it when it was happening. You knew when you had developed a rhythm for the work: you could feel it deep within you, and it felt good.

Sometimes Isaac wanted to tell people that even with all the changes going on in farming, he still liked to do things the old way, like picking cucumbers by hand. He liked to be close to the land. Picking cucumbers made him feel a part of something bigger than himself, something difficult to explain to people.

Isaac and Jake

Isaac thought about his neighbor, Jake Stewart, and his thirty acres of cucumbers. *You can't be close to the land when you farm a thousand acres and grow thirty acres of cucumbers,* Isaac thought.

At the end of the first row, Isaac stood up, stretched out his back, and glanced over to the house. He hadn't seen Jake Stewart's big Buick drive into his yard. Jake was lumbering toward the pickle patch, leaning forward as was his way of walking.

"Howdy, Jake," Isaac said as his old friend got closer.

"Ain't you a little old to be pickin' cukes?" Jake said by way of greeting.

"Still kind of like doin' it," Isaac said. "Honest work."

"I keep tellin' ya, you oughta expand your operation, say put in ten acres, maybe fifteen acres, and get some Mexicans to do the pickin'. Helluva lot easier to have Mexicans out there sweatin' than you doin' it. You know I got myself thirty acres of cukes now; them vines stretch out as far as you can see."

"I've seen your pickle fields, Jake. Look purty good."

"Yup, Mexicans are out there right now. Sight to see, all of them scattered all up and down the field. Little ones, big ones, young ones, old ones. Men, women, kids. They're all out there. Even got a pregnant woman out there pickin'. Everybody in the family 'cept a toddler. Little tyke is out there too, sittin' in the shade and diggin' in the dirt.

"Bet you got a bunch of money stuck in those pickle fields."

"Yeah, I do. But the Harlow people have been helpful. Specially that J. W. Johnson fella. He's been out to the place at least a half-dozen times, checkin' up on things, makin' sure everything is going in the right direction. Got good help from the university in Madison, too. Sent out one of their cucumber men. All the guy does is study cucumbers. Pretty cushy job, but he had some good ideas about how much fertilizer I should be using, stuff like that."

"Hope it works out for you, Jake." Isaac took off his hat and wiped his forehead. He'd heard all this before, but he was trying to be patient with his old friend.

"It's the only way, Isaac. You either get big or you get out. Harlow Company says that. University people say that. These little pickle patches—no offense, Isaac—are a thing of the past. They're history."

"Let's hope not, Jake."

"You are one bullheaded old bastard, Isaac," Jake said, smiling. "You got yourself stuck in yesterday. You'll sit here in the past, and the world is gonna march right past you, run right over you."

"Maybe so, Jake. Maybe so." Isaac wished he could talk with his friend about the importance of the land, about how if you farmed a thousand acres it became impossible to take care of it right. "Jake, you ever hear the saying 'the frog doesn't drink up the pond he lives in'?"

"No, can't say that I have. But what's a frog pond got to do with the size of a pickle patch?" Jake was looking off in the distance as he spoke.

"Everything," Isaac said. "Just about everything."

"You goin' senile on me, Isaac?" Jake turned to Isaac with a broad grin on his face.

"When you got big debts, you expect the land to produce no matter what—and you start abusing it, using it up."

"You accusing me of abusing the land?" Jake asked. His smile was gone, and now he was bristling.

"Just making a comment, that's all. If the shoe fits, wear it."

Isaac and Jake

Both men stood quiet, staring down at the ground. Isaac wished he hadn't brought up the frog in the pond business. He had known Jake since they were both old enough to figure out who was who and what was what. They had gone through grade school and high school together. Their fathers had farmed as neighbors; so had their grandfathers. And they were still farming next to each other. But Jake had gotten caught up in the "you better get bigger" craze. Buy more land. Buy more tractors. Plant more corn. Plant more potatoes. And grow thirty acres of cucumbers. Whoever thought that anybody would grow thirty acres of cucumbers? One farmer with that many acres of cukes? It made no sense to Isaac.

8

Migrant Pickers

Carlos Rodríguez guided his 1950 red Ford flatbed truck slowly down the trail that cut through one of Jake Stewart's big cucumber fields. Carlos, who had just turned forty-five, was stocky, and had a thick black mustache and a ready smile. Carlos had been born in Brownsville, Texas, and grew up traveling north each summer with his family and then returning to Texas for the winter. So he knew the migrant life.

After he married, he continued coming north each summer to work in the cucumber fields. Mostly he enjoyed the life, seeing different parts of the country and especially being paid the money he and his wife and children made picking cucumbers in central Wisconsin. He wanted his children to have a good education and nice clothing and perhaps find less demanding work when they became adults. Working ten-hour days bending over a row of spiny green cucumbers was hard work, no denying it. Carlos, along with most migrant workers, believed strongly that with hard work you got ahead. The Rodríguez family included Carlos's obviously pregnant wife and their three sons, ages fourteen, twelve, and ten. Their three-year-old daughter played nearby while the rest of the family picked cucumbers.

As Carlos drove along the field road watching his sons load bags of cucumbers, he remembered when he was their age. He had worked alongside his father, his brothers, and his sisters picking cherries in Door County, Wisconsin, and then helping with the cucumber harvest in the central part of the state. Cherry picking was easier than picking cucumbers. You didn't have to bend over to pull ripe red cherries from a tree. And cherries didn't stain your hands either. At least not the way those cucumbers did. Picking cucumbers crusted your fingers with a greenish brown stain that only Lava soap would remove, but never completely. By the end of the cucumber season, your fingers looked like the cucumbers you were picking, without the spines, of course.

Carlos had a dream that he hadn't shared with anyone, not even his wife. He wanted to live in the north year-round, to find a job where he and his family didn't have to make the annual trek from Texas to the cucumber fields of central Wisconsin. Few people outside his family knew he was a good cook, but he often thought about opening a restaurant, perhaps in Willow River. The restaurant would serve authentic Mexican food. He knew he would have steady customers in the summer, and he also knew that once the locals became acquainted with his food, they would like it.

Or, even better, he dreamed of working for one of the big pickle companies like H. J. Heinz; Libby, McNeil and Libby; or even the H. H. Harlow Company. He could serve as a connecting link between the farmers, the migrants, and the company. He knew how to talk to farmers, and even better, he knew how to get along with them. And he could solve many farmer–migrant problems when they erupted. Carlos had never heard of a former migrant working for one of these companies, so he didn't tell anyone about his dream. But that didn't keep him from thinking about it.

Migrant Pickers

On that same day, Dewey John, editor of the *Link Lake Gazette*, drove over to a Willow River migrant camp in eastern Ames County. He was gathering information for a story about migrant workers in the county. The Willow River–area cucumber growers had employed migrants for several years, and Jake Stewart's migrants were the first ones employed in western Ames County.

Dewey John was tall, thin, balding, and wore thick glasses that often slid to the end of his oversized nose. He was never seen without his clipboard and papers on which he was constantly making notes. Dewey, a Wisconsin farm boy, had been twenty-eight years old when he drove his green 1949 Ford coupe into the Village of Link Lake on a June morning in 1951. He had been hired as the new editor of the paper, which meant being reporter and photographer and doing whatever else needed doing at this small paper that covered western Ames County. He had been writing for weekly newspapers since he graduated from the University of Wisconsin School of Journalism in 1945. The paper's owner had selected him because of his interest in agriculture and previous experience with country newspapers.

Before driving to the migrant camp, Dewey had done his homework. He learned that the migrants, whom everyone called "Mexicans," were really from southern Texas. Most migrant families spent winters at their homes and worked the harvests in the north during the summer. He learned that they arrived in central Wisconsin in mid-July and helped harvest cucumbers until the end of the season, usually mid-September.

As he pulled into the migrant camp, he saw that it consisted of several small tar-paper–covered buildings clustered at one end of a cornfield, with no shade anywhere. Weeds grew up around these shanties and pushed between the steps leading to the doors.

Three outhouses stood behind them, and the pungent smell wafting from them hit Dewey when he stepped out of his car. A toddler played in a mud puddle just to the side of the rutted trail that led to the shacks. The little boy smiled at him when he walked past.

The workers had stopped picking cucumbers for their noon break, and were sitting in the shade of the shacks, resting. Dewey found several who spoke English, but they didn't have much to say. He told them he was working on a story for the *Link Lake Gazette* about migrant workers.

The migrants lived in these little buildings, sometimes four or five or more in one room, where they cooked and slept with no privacy whatsoever. One woman, dark-haired, friendly, and a little more talkative, upon hearing Dewey was a newspaperman, invited him inside for a look around. The building, obviously hastily constructed, had a door that didn't close completely and one cracked window that didn't open; the air inside was stifling. She said she lived in this one room with her husband and four kids. It was clean and tidy but so cramped he didn't see how they could manage. She said he could take some pictures if he wanted to, as long as no member of her family appeared in any of them.

Dewey talked to the owner of the farm, Fred Ulrich. Ulrich huffed on about how these migrants really liked where they stayed, never complained, and worked hard for him. "Don't know what I'd do without them," Ulrich said. "Nobody can pick cucumbers like these Mexicans."

He wondered if there was more to the story that neither side was sharing. He decided that since Jake Stewart now had migrants, he could talk with him and maybe learn a little more. He headed over to Jake Stewart's farm. As he drove he thought about what he had seen. It seemed Fred Ulrich was taking advantage of his workers. However, none of the migrants he talked with complained; they seemed happy to work for Ulrich.

Jesús Moreno, whom Carlos had recruited from Brownsville, had come north with the Rodríguez family. Jesús helped Carlos's oldest son hoist brown burlap bags of cucumbers onto the truck while the other two boys arranged the bags on the truck bed. Jesús was tall and thin, in his twenties, wore a wide-brimmed straw cowboy hat, and had hair as black as a moonless night. He had dark, cold eyes that could stare right through you. He had but one reason for coming north: the money. He hated the living conditions, didn't like the north, detested the way that some northern people talked to him, and couldn't wait to travel back to Texas. But money was a strong attraction, and he knew that the harder he worked the more money he would earn.

If the crop was good, the weather held, and the prices stayed up—all big ifs—Jesús could earn as much as thirty or more dollars a day. No work in his hometown in Texas would come close to bringing in that kind of money. So he worked hard and kept his anger to himself. Carlos would keep a portion of Jesús's earnings for transporting him to Wisconsin and for finding work and housing for him—Jesús had agreed to this arrangement before he agreed to come.

For the first picking of the season, the farm owner gave the migrants all of the money for the cucumbers. This first picking was difficult because the migrants were expected to train the cucumber vines—steer the plant runners back into the rows, which would make succeeding pickings easier.

Carlos and his family had been picking since daybreak, when the dew was still on the vines. The moisture wet their pants and arms as they worked their way down the long rows, first filling pails and then dumping the cucumbers into burlap bags. The bags were soon lined up across the field, one after the other.

Honeybees buzzed everywhere, visiting the deep-yellow cucumber blossoms in search of nectar. "The better the crop of bees, the better the crop of cucumbers," J. W. Johnson had said when he visited the field and noted all the bees working. The pickers and the bees ignored each other. The bees busily collected nectar; the migrants, cucumbers. The bees stung few cucumber pickers, unless a picker accidentally touched one. "Leave them bees alone, and they'll leave you alone," Johnson had warned.

Mosquitoes, however, bit the pickers unmercifully, especially on hot, humid days with no breeze. The cucumber rows at the edges of the fields were strung out along thick vegetation where the mosquitoes hid. As the day warmed and a little breeze came up, the mosquitoes disappeared, but then the hot summer sun became the enemy. It was a paradox; the cucumbers needed the sun to grow well, but picking them on sunny days, especially at midday, was a miserable experience.

In midmorning Jake Stewart stopped by the cucumber fields. He walked over to Carlos, busy picking on one of the long rows.

"Carlos," Jake said to get his attention.

"Sí, Señor Jake."

"Could you call your family and Jesús together so I could have a word with them?" Jake carried a little book in his hand. It was a Berlitz English-to-Spanish dictionary. While everyone was gathering around him, he paged through it until he found the page he was looking for.

Everyone stood around Jake, wondering what the owner of these vast cucumber fields wanted.

Jake bent over and picked a couple of little cucumbers off the vine in front of him, the size that would be graded number one.

"I want you to . . . ," he hesitated and glanced at the little dictionary where he had underlined the appropriate words, which he badly mangled when he spoke them, "Escoja los pequeños pepinos."

The group stared at him with no response.

"Why don't you just say, 'Be sure to pick the little pickles,'" Carlos said.

"Oh, sure," Jake said surprised. "Yeah, pick the little ones, the money is in the little cukes. Pick the little ones. Ones like these. He held up the two little cucumbers he had in his hand.

"Sí," said Jesús. "We know to peek the leetle peekles. Carlos told us."

"Oh, good," said Jake. "Good, good." He shoved the little dictionary into his back pocket.

"That's all. That's all I wanted," he said.

"Thank you, Señor Jake," Carlos said, motioning everyone back to work. They were all smiling as they resumed picking and Jake got back in his truck and drove away. Jesús was muttering under his breath in Spanish, "Horse's ass, that Señor Jake, trying to speak Spanish." Carlos didn't hear Jesús; he was pleased when people tried to speak his native tongue.

As the morning sun grew hotter, the vines dried and sweat poured down the faces of the migrant pickers, stinging their eyes and soaking their shirts. But not one of them complained, even though the work was hard and the hours long.

Carlos picked on a row near where Jesús was working. He didn't know much about Jesús Moreno. He didn't know that last summer Jesús had come to Wisconsin with a big crew consisting of several families and single men. They had worked the cucumber fields in nearby Portage County. One day, a fellow migrant accused Jesús of claiming more sacks of cucumbers than he had picked. A fight quickly started, knives flashed in the sun, and before the boss could put a stop to it, blood poured from the side of the other man. The Portage County sheriff came by but made no arrests. None of the pickers claimed to have seen anything—they were all busy picking cucumbers. What the sheriff had was Jesús and the wounded migrant, each claiming the other was at fault. Finally, he told the migrant boss to keep his men from killing each other, and that was the last of it. The wounded man had spent several days recovering in a Stevens Point hospital.

What Carlos did know was that Jesús always carried a sharp folding knife in his pocket, which wasn't that unusual. And he also knew that he was a loner. Whenever the family had stopped along the way when they were driving north, Jesús sat off by himself, saying little, opening and closing his knife or just staring off into space. But he was a good worker; he filled as many sacks with cucumbers as did Carlos.

Later that afternoon, Carlos slowly drove his truck across the cucumber field as the young men loaded burlap bags filled with cucumbers. María and their little girl walked to their living quarters. Before the season, Jake Stewart had cleaned out a shed that had been used for storage. He dragged out some old horse-drawn implements—a one-horse cultivator, a walking plow—parts from an old grain binder, and a hunk of canvas that mice had chewed big holes in. He dumped the entire lot behind the shed, swept down the cobwebs, cleaned the dirt and grime as best he could from the concrete floor, and declared it livable.

"They don't need much for these few weeks in the summer," Jake had answered when his daughter, Amy, said the shed didn't look like a place where people could live.

He had found some old beds and mattresses, bought a second-hand kerosene stove, and set up a makeshift sink with a pipe that spilled outside on the ground. A few yards away stood an old out-house that Jake had abandoned when the Stewarts got indoor plumbing a year ago.

When the Rodríguezes had arrived with an extra young man, Jake swept out the brooder house for him, a little building he had once used to raise baby chicks. There was a mouse hole in one corner of the building, and the wooden door had a missing board. Jake dragged in an old canvas cot he'd gotten as army surplus. When he finished cleaning, he stood back, quite proud of the ac-commodations he had prepared for his first-ever crew of cucum-ber pickers.

He had shown the facilities to J. W. Johnson, who had said, "Looks purty good to me. Yup, I think your Mexicans will be right comfortable. Don't want to treat 'em too good, you know. Harlow folks tell me you gotta keep 'em in their place."

Dewey John arrived at Jake Stewart's place in time to see the migrants loading the truck. "Mind if I talk to them?" He had asked Jake.

"Nah, go right ahead. But don't get in their way. They got work to do. Got at least a couple loads of cukes to haul to the pickle factory 'fore it gets dark," Jake said.

"Hello," Carlos said, when he saw the man with a clipboard approaching. Carlos stopped his truck.

"I'm with the local newspaper," Dewey said. "May I ask you some questions?"

"Sí," Carlos answered.

Carlos and Dewey chatted for a few minutes, as the latter gathered more information for his Ames County migrant worker story. The Rodríguez boys gathered around to listen in, but not Jesús Moreno. He said something to Carlos in Spanish and began walking to the far end of the field.

It was early evening when the men had the truck fully loaded; Jesús and the Rodríguez boys hopped on the back, on top of the cucumber sacks, and Carlos slowly drove back across the field. He turned onto the dirt road that trailed by the Stewart farm, shifted gears as he picked up speed, and headed toward Link Lake and the pickle factory. Jake had given him careful directions on how to find it.

Heads turned as the truck drove by farmsteads on its way into town.

"Wonder who that is, and what he's haulin'?"

"Guys on that truck don't look like they're from around here."

"Kinda looks like it might be bags of cucumbers on that truck, but where in God's creation did they find a whole truckload?"

Carlos slowed the truck and turned into the drive that led to the pickle factory. Blackie Antonelli stood outside, motioning him to drive up alongside an area where two big doors stood open and a large piece of green machinery was visible on an elevated platform.

9

Unloading

J. W. Johnson and Andy stood on the main floor and watched as the big truck from the Stewart farm backed up to the pickle factory door. Johnson's armpits were wet, and sweat poured off his face. Late in the day the humidity had come up, and there was no breeze, nor hint of one, in the valley where the pickle factory was located.

"Good God, that's a bunch of cukes," Blackie said. "Never saw that many come here at one time."

"Got our work cut out for us tonight," Agnes said quietly.

Jesús and the Rodríguez boys jumped down off the truck and quickly began dragging and lifting bag after heavy bag of cucumbers to the unloading platform.

For a moment, the pickle factory crew just stared because they had never seen migrant workers before, never heard anyone speak Spanish, never seen people with dark skin.

Quarter Mile Sweet and Blackie Antonelli began untying each bag and dumping the cucumbers onto the sorter. Sweat dripped from all the men, running into their eyes and soaking their shirts. But they didn't stop, didn't even slow down.

Unloading

Not stopping to rest may have had something to do with an un-spoken competition, pickle factory guys versus Mexicans. Neither Mexicans nor factory workers wanted to slow down or even sug-gest that they couldn't take the hard work, the heat, and the hu-midity. So they sweated, and in the process eyed each other, watch-ing how each other worked, used their hands, lifted—looking for differences but not finding any.

Agnes Swarsinski hovered over the vibrating sorter like a mother hen watching her brood. Cucumbers bounced across the sorter, the little ones dropping through the narrow slots and tumbling into wooden crates first, the larger ones working their way along the jerking sorter, falling into their designated chan-nels. Agnes searched for imperfection, a badly deformed cucum-ber, evidence of disease, rot, or mold—anything out of the ordi-nary. But she saw nothing as wave after wave of green passed before her eyes. She watched the young migrants and Quarter Mile and Blackie eyeing each other but not saying a word, and she thought of strange dogs that come together and circle each other sniffing and prancing, looking, growling a little, but not too much. Showing their teeth on occasion.

Preacher carried each wooden bushel crate to the scale—box upon box full of number threes and number fours, fewer boxes of number twos, and fewer boxes still of gherkins. Soon his shirt was wet and sweat dripped from his brow. He was not accustomed to heavy physical work, and he grunted each time he lifted a box. He probably didn't even know he was doing it, but Agnes heard it and turned to look for the source of the sound. Andy Meyer heard it too but said nothing. He worked the scale, moved the brass indi-cator back and forth until the scale arm balanced, and then wrote the numbers on a pad. Then he put down the pad and pencil and helped Preacher lift the bushel crates of cucumbers from the scale to a four-wheeled cart that would tote them to the vats for salting, a job that the crew would do later that evening.

When he had a pad full of numbers, Andy carried the sheet to the office where Helen Swanson started two tallies, one for a check to Jake Stewart and one for a check to Carlos Rodríguez, half the total to each. Carlos had jotted down the number of bags of cucumbers Jesús had picked, and he would pay him accordingly. And as per their agreement that the migrants would receive all the income from the first picking, Jake would endorse his first check to Carlos.

It took nearly an hour to unload Jake's load of cucumbers. While they waited for Helen to prepare the checks, Carlos and Andy talked. It was the first time that Andy had talked to a migrant worker—in fact it was the first time he had been this close to one. Andy was surprised that Carlos seemed like any other person—skin a bit darker and hair blacker than most people Andy knew, but a friendly fellow with an easy grin.

Andy told him that in the three years he had worked at the pickle factory, this was the largest amount of cucumbers they had ever taken in at one time. Carlos talked about Jake Stewart's cucumber fields and how good the crop was this year.

Meanwhile, Quarter Mile and Blackie and the young Mexicans were still circling each other and sniffing. "You speak English?" Quarter Mile asked, looking Jesús Moreno in the eye.

"Sí, we speak English," answered Jesús.

"People call me Quarter Mile; my real name is Paul."

"I am Jesús, Jesús Moreno," the young Mexican said. He pronounced it "Hay-soos."

"How do you spell that?"

The young migrant spelled, "J-e-s-u-s."

"Hey, that spells Jesus," Blackie Antonelli piped in. "For God's sake, you got the same name as Christ?"

"Sí," said Jesús Moreno. "But you say 'hay-soos.'"

"Sure as hell is a dumb name," Blackie said, walking away and leaving Quarter Mile with the young migrants.

"He got a problem with me?" Jesús asked, bristling.

"Nah, Blackie's like that," Quarter Mile said.

Helen came out of the little office and handed the payment to Carlos Rodríguez. The migrant workers got back in the truck without another word. The red truck drove up the drive and disappeared into the twilight.

"Seems like a good time to eat supper," Andy said as he pulled up an empty cucumber crate and opened his lunch bucket. The rest of the factory crew grabbed their lunch buckets as well, except for Helen, who was working at her desk in the office.

"Before we eat, we must have a word of prayer," Preacher said.

"Let us bow our heads." Everyone was so taken by surprise that they stopped unwrapping their sandwiches and did as he asked.

"Heavenly Father," he began, "we are gathered together this evening in a place of your creation; we are gathered among the fruits of the harvest, this wonderful bounty of cucumbers. We are gathered as workers celebrate this work and thank you for the meal we are about to receive. We are gathered . . ."

"For Christ's sake, I want to eat, not pray," Blackie Antonelli interrupted, jumping to his feet. "Godammit, this is a pickle factory, not a church. What in hell has got in to you all? You takin' up religion?"

"Young man," Preacher said quietly. "I am offended by your comments, and your ill-advised profanity."

"By God, it's high time you heard a little swearing, Preacher. It's about time you did. This here is a pickle factory, and some of us cuss on occasion. And we don't sit around and pray before we eat. We sure as hell don't do that."

Preacher got to his feet, picked up his lunch bucket, and said, "I will eat my supper with Helen." With that, he walked off to the office where Helen had taken out her sandwich and was unwrapping it.

"Pipe down, Blackie, he's a preacher. Preachers pray," Andy said.

"I don't give a shit who he is. No preacher is gonna get me to pray in this pickle factory," Blackie said.

The remainder of the crew chuckled as they unwrapped their lunches.

"Speaking of religion, you know the difference between a Baptist and a Methodist?" Agnes asked.

"Don't think I do," said Quarter Mile.

"Baptists don't wave at each other in a liquor store."

Hoots of laughter all around as the crew ate their sandwiches.

Andy wondered how this crew would come together. He knew it sometimes took a few days for people to get to know each other, to find out each other's quirks and strange doings. What mattered most was that they sorted cucumbers and salted them away each evening. They didn't have to like each other.

10

Long Days

The *Link Lake Gazette* ran a front-page story about Jake's pickle fields and the migrants he had in his employ. John wrote about the shacks where they lived and how crowded they were. He had expected letters or phone calls from *Gazette* readers, but none came. So far the community didn't seem to care that migrants lived and worked at Jake Stewart's place or what their living conditions were.

During the first days in August, the cucumbers continued rolling in to the pickle factory, truckload after truckload from Jake Stewart's thirty acres, and sack after sack from the little cucumber patches found on almost every farm around Link Lake. A couple of timely rains and sunny, hot weather contributed to high yields and happy faces.

The days at the pickle factory were long and tiring. Andy pulled open the doors each morning at eight. Usually the first customers were already waiting, farmers who had picked their patches the previous afternoon and didn't want to wait in line at night. In early evening the truckloads of cucumbers would arrive from Stewart's farm, and no farmer with six gunnysacks of cucumbers and three rambunctious kids wanted to wait an hour for a truckload of cucumbers to be unloaded and sorted before they could unload theirs.

The crew was holding up reasonably well, but as workers grew tired, tempers often flared. So far, Andy was able to keep everyone working, although Blackie Antonelli constantly picked on Quarter Mile Sweet.

"Okay, college boy," Blackie would say. "Bet you can't lift two bushel boxes of cucumbers at the same time." Blackie demonstrated that he could easily lift the 120-plus pounds.

Without responding, mild-mannered Quarter Mile lifted the two boxes and hoisted them over his head to show he was as strong as—or maybe even stronger than—wiry Blackie Antonelli.

Blackie would walk away from such events without commenting, obviously thinking of some other stunt to pull on Quarter Mile, some dirty trick like pushing him into a pickle vat. Andy kept a close watch on the two of them.

Agnes Swarsinski was like a grandma to the crew. She worked hard, took no guff from anyone, and always had a wise comment or a joke to tell.

"Hear about the two men who walked into a bar?" she asked one noon during lunch.

"No, can't say as I did," Andy answered, smiling.

"They both had headaches."

"What?"

"I said they walked into a bar. Didn't say what kind of bar it was."

Whenever they encountered each other, Blackie and Jesús Moreno were like a pair of fighting roosters, each wanting to fly into the other. Back in late July, Blackie had made fun of Jesús's name again, saying he had no right to use the name of Christ for himself.

Jesús bristled, snapped open his folding knife, and made a roundhouse swing at Blackie, who jumped back, grabbing a two-by-four that was leaning against one of the pickle vats. Blackie swung the two-by-four and hit Jesús on the leg, knocking him down. Quickly Jesús scrambled to his feet, his dark eyes wide and menacing, his long, sharp knife poised to catch Blackie in the neck.

While this was going on, both Carlos and Andy were in the office, checking on some delivery figures. Who should step between Jesús and Blackie but frail little Preacher; he just walked right up and stood between them. Both were so surprised that they immediately stopped fighting.

"Get out of the way Preacher, or you'll get yourself killed," Blackie said.

"I am a man of the cloth, a man of peace," Preacher said quietly. "Violence solves nothing."

Catholic Jesús Moreno would pick a fight with anyone, but he had great respect for preachers and priests.

"You two cool off and go back to work. Put away that knife, and park that two-by-four," Preacher said.

The young men did as he ordered. From that day on the crew at the pickle factory had new respect for the quiet man who had insisted on praying before they ate their meals. But they also wondered if something was going on between him and Helen; since the incident about praying before their supper, Preacher ate both his noon and evening meals with Helen, in her office or outside in the shade of the factory. Andy had heard that Preacher was counseling Helen, and she did seem more cheerful as the weeks wore on. Andy appreciated that Helen was no longer coming to work crying or crying on the job. And through it all, not once had she let up on her work. Not one of the reports that she filled out—payroll records, salt records—came back from J. W. Johnson's office with errors noted. Johnson had earlier commented that the bookkeeper at the pickle factory in Willow River was a dud. Nearly every week a report had to be corrected. Once an entire vat of cucumbers there had been salted improperly, and the higher-ups in Chicago had to figure how they could save the hundreds of bushels of cucumbers in the vat—all gherkins, too. Johnson said he wished he had a bookkeeper like Helen at Willow River.

Helen began attending Preacher's church services on Sunday mornings. She had asked for Sunday mornings off, and Andy had said he could write the few checks from the handful of growers that brought in their cucumbers on Sunday mornings. Helen was always back promptly at noon with a big smile on her face.

There were still about six weeks left before the cucumber season would wind down and the factory would close. Andy kept his fingers crossed that he could keep everything together, keep the workers from fighting with each other, and keep Jesús and Blackie from killing one another.

Carlos Rodríguez had heard all the details of the fight between cocky Jesús Moreno and hotheaded Blackie Antonelli. Like Andy, the last thing he wanted was conflict between the migrants and the locals. One August evening, after the last sack of cucumbers had been dumped into the sorter, he retrieved a bottle from the front seat of his truck and passed it around, suggesting everyone take a drink.

The crew, with the exception of Preacher, usually enjoyed a can of beer or a snort of whiskey toward the end of a shift. But when they took a mouthful of the clear liquid being passed around, they knew they'd tasted something different and more powerful than anything they had ever swallowed.

"Tastes like kerosene; burns when it goes down," Agnes Swarsinski said as she passed the bottle on to Quarter Mile Sweet. She was shaking her head back and forth. Quarter Mile took a big swallow, coughed, swallowed hard, and tried to hide the fact that his eyes were watering. Preacher took a smell of the bottle. "Devil's drink," he pronounced and passed it on to Helen Swanson, who took a big drink, swallowed it, and took another drink.

"Are you staying, Helen?" Preacher asked. He couldn't believe that she would drink from a bottle being passed around. "I'm heading on home."

"Good stuff," she said, in a whisper, as the drink had taken away her breath. "I think I'll stay a little while."

"Tequila," Carlos said. "Tequila from Mexico. Good, huh?" He smiled broadly as the bottle went around a second time.

Soon the migrants and the pickle factory crew were laughing and sharing stories. Carlos talked about what it was like to be a migrant and travel around the country. The pickle factory crew listened intently, for none of them had ever been out of Wisconsin, except Agnes, who had once visited some of her relatives in Chicago.

It was after midnight when Andy dumped the last bushel of cucumbers into its appropriate vat and added the salt and water. He hoped that Helen had figured the salt correctly.

When Andy arrived at the pickle factory the next morning a half-hour late, he saw Preacher setting on the steps, reading his Bible.

"Good morning," Andy said. His head was throbbing.

"Good morning to you, Andy, and what a beautiful morning it is," Preacher answered.

"Oh, yes, it is a nice morning," Andy muttered.

The rest of the crew staggered in shortly after. Andy did not scold anyone for being late.

11

Pickle Days

In 1948 the city fathers had decided that they needed something to attract people to the area, to give local businesses a boost and, as the village president said, "Put Link Lake on the map." They agreed to erect a statue—something that would stand out and make Link Lake a special place to visit. But what kind? Should it be a huge Holstein (most farmers owned cows), a giant sandbur (these pesky weeds were everywhere), a bundle of wheat (the area once grew acres of it), or a statue of Increase Joseph Link (the pioneer pastor who founded the town in 1852)? After weeks of deliberation, the decision leaned toward a statue of Increase Joseph. That is, until a representative of the H. H. Harlow Pickle Company stepped forward and said that Harlow would cover the cost if the town erected a cucumber sculpture. Faster than you could say "Mother Harlow knows pickles," the city fathers decided, unanimously, to install a giant cucumber.

Now the challenge was to find someone to build the statue. They all agreed it should be made of wood, because that would be the cheapest. The committee chairman, John Dobrey (the local undertaker and furniture store owner), started looking for a carpenter to build the big cucumber. Dobrey soon discovered that finding someone qualified to construct a thirty-foot-tall cucumber was not easy. When he found a couple of local carpenters he thought might be up to it, they turned him down. They said they were accustomed to building straight things, and clearly there was nothing straight about a cucumber.

With a stroke of genius, Dobrey thought to contact a builder of farm silos, a fellow from Westfield, one Alphonse Steinnecker. Silos were, of course, cylindrical, as was a cucumber, at least somewhat. After considerable thought, Steinnecker took on the project and spent most of a summer measuring, sawing, pounding, forming, shaving, and sanding until he had a monster cucumber erected on a concrete platform with three concrete steps leading up to it. "You gotta have a firm foundation for an artistic work like this," he proclaimed. "And you can quote me on that." The immense green cucumber replica stood on one end of Main Street, on a little hill that overlooked the lake.

Not everyone agreed it looked like a cucumber, especially during the construction phase. Some said it resembled a ruptured blimp that had landed on its end and kind of crumpled in the middle. Others said it looked like an enormous Polish sausage. A couple of young guys leaving the Link Lake Tap one Saturday night came face-to-face with the near completed sculpture and said, "Looks like what Paul Bunyan's dog would leave behind."

Of course it was the latter comment that made the rounds of Link Lake and set tongues to wagging about whether they'd made a huge mistake asking Steinnecker to build something he'd never built before, no matter how firm its foundation.

When Alphonse finished the carpentry work, he leaned an extension ladder against the structure and began painting it green.

Opinions began changing. Especially when he painted the black spots representing the cucumber's spines.

"Yup, looks like a cucumber. Sort of, anyway," an onlooker said.

Two nights after the structure began looking like a cucumber, a wicked thunderstorm blew across Link Lake and fiercely buffeted the new sculpture. In the clear light of morning, Link Lake citizens noted that their new attraction leaned to the northeast several degrees, but was otherwise unharmed. No one could figure out how to straighten it, so forever after it was fondly called the Leaning Pickle of Link Lake. A plaque, screwed firmly to its base, read, "Donated by the H. H. Harlow Pickle Company, in commemoration of the importance of cucumbers to the community of Link Lake, Wisconsin, 1948."

It made sense for the community to follow with the sponsorship of Link Lake Pickle Days. The annual celebration was a way for the community to show off its big cucumber, and Pickle Days soon became its most important celebration. The American Legion sponsored a second-rate parade on Memorial Day, and the community sponsored a short fireworks display on the Fourth of July, but clearly the town saved its energy for Pickle Days. Some said more people attended Pickle Days than the Ames County Fair at Willow River. That was probably an exaggeration, but people did come from miles around to take part in all the hoopla centered on the lowly cucumber, and to see the big green statue.

Extended families that saw each other perhaps only at Christmas gathered during Pickle Days. Main Street store owners decorated their windows with green bunting. The Ames County Art and Photographer's Society held its annual competition on Pickle Days weekend, and all entries depicted cucumbers in some way.

Society members prominently displayed their work in the various store windows for all to see for several weeks leading up to Pickle Days. The displays included paintings and photographs of cucumber fields, the leaning pickle statue, people picking cucumbers, little children holding cucumbers, even the Harlow pickle factory. This year, a blue ribbon was tied to a painting of an enormous cucumber leaning against a big oak tree, with a smiling farmer standing next to it. The caption read, "We grow them big in Ames County." The painting was proudly displayed in the Link Lake Mercantile window.

Pickle Days meant money for the local businesses; they all supported the celebration and planned for it months in advance. Businesses included the Link Lake Mercantile: "Buy your overalls, Wolverine shoes, six-buckle rubber boots, and groceries all under one roof"; Link Lake Grist Mill: "You bring it and we'll grind it"; Johnson's Hardware: "If you've lost a nut, come see us"; Amery's Clothing Store: "Our long underwear does not itch"; Sven's leather shop: "We repair soles"; Link Lake Motors: "Your local Ford dealer"; Wendell's Mobil gas station with the Flying Red Horse: "You need gas, we got it"; Dobrey's Furniture Store and Mortuary: "We are here in your time of need"; the Link Lake Cheese Factory: "Standalone Limburger cheese our specialty." And of course there was the Link Lake Tap, which was consistently criticized but always filled with customers, especially on weekends.

The *Link Lake Gazette*'s office was tucked between Sven's leather shop and Korman's Restaurant. The *Gazette* regularly ran editorials reminding people to shop at home and resist driving to Stevens Point, Oshkosh, Berlin, or Willow River when they needed something. "Is it worth losing a local business by saving a quarter on a pair of pants purchased in Oshkosh?" "Is it worth seeing the grist mill close because you thought you could save a dollar by hauling your grain to Willow River or Waupaca for grinding? On a snowy day in winter, when you are forced to drive twenty miles on slippery roads to have your cow feed ground, you will wish you had frequented the local mill."

Link Lake celebrated Pickle Days the first weekend of August, in the peak of the cucumber harvest season. The parade on Saturday afternoon drew the most people, followed by the "Big Pickle Polka Dance" on Saturday night. Of course, that morning, everyone gathered to watch the local cucumber judging in a tent set up in the parking lot in back of the Link Lake Mercantile. The competition for best cucumber in the area was keen, with a traveling plaque in the shape of a huge green, spiny cucumber going to the winner. Last year Isaac Meyer had won the award, but some people griped that he shouldn't even have entered his cucumbers, what with his son, Andy, managing the pickle factory. Andy had nothing to do with the contest; in fact, he didn't go near the judging tent, but people talked nonetheless.

This year Jake Stewart had his eye on the prize and the fame that accompanied it. With thirty acres to select from, he figured he would easily be named the pickle champion of Link Lake. The Ames County agricultural agent and J. W. Johnson judged the event. After much deliberation, Jake Stewart was declared the pickle champion of Link Lake for 1955. "Best cucumbers I've seen in a long time," declared Johnson.

The pickle factory opened as usual that Saturday, with a few pickup loads of cucumbers arriving before ten o'clock. Nobody wanted to miss the Pickle Parade. Main Street was already packed full by mid–Saturday morning. The town marshal, Justin Quick, wearing a bright green shirt commemorating the day, closed the street at eleven for the parade. That same hour, Andy shut down the pickle factory. He would open it again at two and then close it at six so everyone could go to the dance on Main Street. Andy changed into his army uniform, which he'd brought along that morning, and headed down to where the tractors, horses, floats, a band, and other parade participants were gathering.

Andy was looking forward to a few hours away from the pickle factory. Even better, Amy Stewart was coming home for the weekend; he hadn't seen her since his father's birthday party back in June. Andy and Amy had exchanged only a couple of letters since her last time home; he was too busy at the pickle factory to do much letter writing, and she was obviously wrapped up with her job at J. I. Case. He hoped they could have some long talks and perhaps even make some plans.

The Link Lake fire station's whistle blew promptly at twelve, as it did every day. The crowd cheered and the parade began. The reviewing stand had been erected in front of the leaning pickle statue at the end of Main Street, and there sat the village president and the village board members. When the parade reached the reviewing stand, it veered right down First Street and on to the village park near the lake.

Marshal Quick led the parade, riding a big white horse that walked with its head high and danced on all four legs because the animal was not accustomed to large crowds. "Whoa, easy boy," Marshal Quick said as the horse pranced down Main Street.

Members of the American Legion followed. They marched mostly in a straight line, carrying M-1 rifles on their shoulders. Andy Meyer marched in front, limping slightly and carrying the American flag. He proudly led the small troop of Link Lake war heroes and veterans from World War I, World War II, and the Korean Conflict.

A horse-drawn float, a hay wagon covered with green and white crepe paper, came next. The 1955 pickle queen, Gloria Jean Patterson, wearing a green off-the-shoulder gown, a gold sash that read "Pickle Queen," and a crown resembling a cucumber plant, rode on the wagon with her court. The pickle court consisted of four young women all dressed in beautiful green gowns. They sat on hay bales and smiled and waved to the crowd.

Little Cynthia Adams, the Gherkin Princess (winner of a competition for girls three to six), sat next to the green-gowned court and queen. Cynthia was a black-haired beauty at age five, with dark eyes and a wide smile. She also wore a green gown and a gold sash, with the words "Gherkin Princess" imprinted on it. She tossed little green cucumber candies to the crowd. The children along the parade route scrambled after the treats.

The big green Link Lake garbage truck rolled down the street next, washed clean and shining, its diesel engine belching smelly black smoke. Next came Link Lake's 1942 fire truck, a vehicle purchased by the city in 1946 as army surplus. Some claimed the truck had a military record. Folks in Link Lake complained that they needed a new one, but the city fathers answered, "With so few fires, this one suits us just fine—besides, the truck is a war hero."

The fire truck blew its siren; children covered their ears, and even the most docile parade horses sidestepped. When the fire truck arrived opposite the mercantile, a volunteer firefighter blew the siren a bit longer than usual. There was a terrific explosion as the old red truck backfired and a cloud of gray smoke shot from the exhaust pipe and settled over the crowd. Then the vehicle shuddered like an injured animal and died without further warning. The driver struggled to start it, but the old iron beast was dead, clear evidence for the "new fire truck is needed" crowd. A half-dozen men came forward, all smiling and laughing, and pushed the fire truck onto a side street so the parade could continue.

Another hay wagon, this one pulled by an orange Allis-Chalmers tractor, followed the ill-fated fire truck. A gold banner was strung across both sides of it, decorated with the words "Salvation Singers: Church of the Holy Redeemed." A pump organ stood on the front of the wagon and Ethel Ketchum, the preacher's wife, sat at the keyboard. Someone later noted that she looked like she would come apart with her arms and legs flying in all directions as she struck the keys and pumped the instrument. Without a smile, without an expression on her face, she played "Nearer My God to Thee" as the wagon slowly rolled down Main Street.

Four large and perspiring middle-aged women wearing flowered, tight-fitting dresses clustered on the wagon, sharing hymnals. Helen Swanson, who had recently joined the church, was the fifth member. Her willowy figure contrasted with those of the big, motherly matrons who surrounded her. Helen smiled broadly as she sang the old church songs familiar to most churchgoers, no matter what their affiliation. Those who listened carefully heard that the Salvation Singers either sang behind Ethel's playing or ahead of her. Neither Ethel nor the singers seemed aware of any difficulties.

J. W. Johnson in his green H. H. Harlow pickup decorated with green bunting came next. He wore a bright green shirt and green cap.

Pickle Days

Jake Stewart, riding in the cab of Carlos Rodríguez's Ford flatbed truck, followed the Harlow entry. His migrant crew sat on the back of the truck among several sacks of cucumbers they had picked that morning. Several old tractors followed the Stewart cucumbers: a F-12 Farmall, all sparkling red; a low-slung gray Fordson with red wheels; an old Rumley Oil pull tractor, a shiny gray and red Ford 8N; and a huge Case steam engine, shooting wood smoke and sparks from its stack. Every few yards the driver pulled the cord, the steam whistle screamed, and little children clung to their mothers.

The Willow River Riding Club rode a dozen Palomino horses with shiny brown coats and blond tails and manes—they pranced down Main Street and left odiferous reminders in their wake. The riders wore buckskin-fringed jackets and big white hats and sat astride black, silver-studded saddles.

A shiny green John Deere B tractor followed, crushing flat the deposits left by the horses in the street. The tractor pulled a hay wagon on which rode Albert Olson strumming his banjo, Thomas John Jones bowing his fiddle, and Louie Pixley fingering a button concertina. They each wore bright green shirts and new-looking straw hats and sat on bales of green alfalfa hay. As the wagon passed the mercantile, the trio played a raucous version of the "Beer Barrel Polka," which brought cheers from the crowd.

Next came the Link Lake Historical Society float. On a flatbed International truck stood a man dressed in black from head to toe. He carried a red book under his arm.

A big sign on each side of the truck read, "Increase Joseph Link: Founder of Link Lake." The old timers in the community knew that the original Link had moved to Wisconsin from New

York State in 1852 with a small band of followers, called the Standalone Fellowship. This religious group established Link Lake and built the Standalone Church, which for years had ministered to the community and challenged those who misused the land.

The Link Lake High School band brought up the rear. Dressed in their purple and gold wool uniforms, twenty perspiring students marched in straight lines as they played "Stars and Stripes Forever." The crowd clapped and cheered as they passed.

Oscar Wilson, a local farmer, and Ole Olson, the miller (who was all cleaned up and thus didn't look at all like himself), stood near the pickle statue.

"Mighty fine parade this year, Ole," Wilson said.

"That it was. That it was," Ole responded.

With the parade over, Marshal Quick removed the barriers and began directing the traffic that had backed up while the parade was in progress.

Andy headed back to the pickle factory. He and the crew worked a few hours in the afternoon, and then Andy closed the factory at six for the evening festivities and headed home to clean up. Marshal Quick blocked off Main Street once more. The members of the three-piece polka band climbed back on their float wagon at about 8:30 and tuned their instruments, and the dance began. Women with full skirts and colorful blouses and men with open-necked shirts and church-going pants danced the polka, the old-time waltz, the two-step, the schottische, and more, on worn pavement designed for automobiles and trucks, not dancers.

Sounds of laughter drifted out the doors of the Link Lake Tap along with the smell of cigarette smoke and stale beer. Kids of all sizes with double-dip ice-cream cones, bags of popcorn, Hershey candy bars, and soft drinks in bottles lined the sidewalk, watching the dancers and looking forward to when they were a little older and could jump up and down in the middle of the street like their older brothers and sisters and their fathers and mothers.

"Put your arms around me honey, hold me tight," the band members sang, and the dancers sang with them. Some of the young people referred to this tune as the "butcher" song— "butcher arms around me honey . . ."

Meanwhile, Andy stopped by the Stewarts' and picked up Amy, who had arrived on the afternoon train. She looked radiant in a bright yellow dress with a green sash.

"It's so good to see you, Andy," she said, squeezing his hand. He smiled and said he was glad to see her, too. She brushed up close to him; the smell of her perfume filled the humid night air. Then she wrapped her arms around his neck and kissed him.

"It's so good to see you," she repeated. Andy smiled. He was looking forward to the evening.

After arriving in Link Lake, Andy and Amy held hands as they walked along Main Street, looking at the various store window displays and talking about Pickle Days of earlier years. The dance music drew them toward the other end of the street.

Soon the two of them were dancing, doing the polka that they both enjoyed, singing along with the band while its members played and sang, "In heaven there is no beer, that's why we drink it here," and then immediately moved into the "So Smart Polka." Perspiration was beading on Andy's forehead as he and Amy danced and sang, "Just because you think you're so pretty, just be-cause you think you're so smart. Just because you think you've got something that nobody else has got."

Now the band shifted to the "Blue Skirt Waltz" and Amy snuggled up to Andy as they sang along with the band: "I dream of that night with you, lady, when first we met. We danced in a world of blue." Next it was "I was dancing with my darling to the Tennessee Waltz." Andy looked into Amy's blue eyes and thought how beautiful she was. He couldn't remember when he'd had so much fun.

Both out of breath, they walked over to the lakefront and sat on a little bench that overlooked a small bay. The moon was climbing above the water, its light reflecting on the dark waters of the lake.

They could hear the band in the distance playing another polka, and the band members singing, "Hoop de do, hoop de do, I hear a polka and my troubles are through." Both Andy and Amy knew the words to the tune.

"Beautiful night," Andy said. Amy put her head on his shoulder as they both looked over the black water with the moonlight dancing on the still surface. Once more she put her arms around him and kissed him. And he kissed her and held her tight.

A slender fellow wearing a white shirt unbuttoned nearly to his waist stumbled along the sidewalk; he obviously had been celebrating a little too much. He stopped near where Andy and Amy were embracing.

"Doin' a little makin' out I see?" the drunk said as he wavered from side to side, nearly falling over before he corrected his lean and moved in the other direction without shifting his feet.

"On your way," Andy said, angrily.

"Jeez, just askin' a polite question, tha's all."

The drunk continued along the sidewalk, staggering from side to side and nearly falling off the curb.

Neither Andy nor Amy said anything for a long time.

"Andy, there's something that's bothering me," Amy finally said.

"On a beautiful night like this? How can anything bother anyone?"

"It's about our fathers," Amy said seriously.

"What about them?"

"Your dad and my dad aren't getting along very well these days."

"I know," Andy said quietly, not wanting to think about the rift that had developed between these lifelong friends.

"Your dad is so stubborn," Amy said.

"Not any more than yours," Andy said, smiling.

"How come your dad is so caught up in doing things the old way?"

"Sometimes the old way is the better way," said Andy.

"Not when it comes to farming."

"Especially when it comes to farming," Andy said. He had stopped smiling.

They sat next to each other, not touching, listening to polka music drift down Main Street: the Pennsylvania Polka and then the Sheboygan Schottische—one-two-three-hop, one-two-three-hop, hop, hop, hop, hop.

"You sound like your dad," Amy said.

"I happen to agree with him. Changing to something new just because it's new is usually a bad idea. Changing how you farm without holding onto what's basic to farming is always a bad idea," Andy said.

"You think that's what my dad is doing?" She raised her voice.

"Yeah, that's what I think he's doing."

"What's basic about farming? It's mostly hard work and never knowing if you'll earn a dollar." Amy had a cynical edge to her voice.

"What's basic is taking care of the land," Andy said, raising his voice more than he intended.

"You think Dad's not taking care of his land?" Amy said. Her face was flushed.

"Yeah, that's what I think."

"Well you are dead wrong, Mr. Andy Meyer. Dead wrong."

"You don't take care of the land by plowing fifty-acre fields, by growing thirty acres of cucumbers, by pouring tons of fertilizer on the fields, by trying to farm a thousand acres," Andy said quietly. He stood up.

"It's the future, Andy. Get big or get out. That's what the university says, that's what the Harlow Pickle Company says, that's what the farm implement companies and the feed companies say. You work for Harlow. Don't you agree with them?"

"They're all wrong, every last one of them, including Harlow." Now Andy raised his voice a little, and his face turned red. "Are you getting your ideas from J. I. Case, who's trying to sell more tractors? Do they really care about farmers?"

The band played the "Rain, Rain Polka," but neither Andy nor Amy heard the music.

"So you think I'm getting my ideas from the Case Company?" Amy asked in a louder than normal voice.

"Yeah, that's what I think."

"Well, maybe I am," she said. Her face was flushed.

"Between your old man and the Case Company you've got yourself a head full of wrong ideas," Andy said angrily. "What happens when a farmer begins buying out his neighbors—we have fewer and fewer farmers. And pretty soon, towns like this start disappearing."

"The good farmers get bigger, the bad farmers sell out," Amy said in a matter-of-fact way.

"So you think my dad is a bad farmer?"

"I didn't say that."

"Sounded like you did."

Amy got up and walked past Andy to the edge of the lake. The band was playing an old-time waltz, and the sound seemed to bounce on the placid, watery surface. Across the lake, a whip-poorwill called its name, over and over.

Amy turned around, walked back to where Andy stood, and said, "Take me home, Andy. I guess we have nothing more to talk about."

"If that's what you want."

"That's what I want."

They didn't talk all the way to the Stewart farm. When she got out of the car, Amy ran to the house. Andy saw she was crying.

12

Cucumbers Keep Coming

The Monday following Pickle Days, Andy sat at the kitchen table reading the *Link Lake Gazette*. His mother was working in the dining room, and his father was outside somewhere. He'd have to leave for the pickle factory in a few minutes. Then he noticed the big ad the Harlow Company ran every week.

> Mother Harlow's pickles. When you want the best you ask for Mother Harlow. Farm grown. Kitchen tested. Quality assured. Even kids like Mother Harlow's dill pickles.

Most of the ad was accurate, he thought, especially the quality part. He worked hard to help Harlow maintain high quality. He wasn't so sure about the part claiming that kids like Harlow dill pickles. He remembered not liking dill pickles when he was a kid, not even the ones his mother prepared.

He read the mercantile's much smaller ad:

Link Lake Mercantile

25 pounds sugar—$2.38
1 pound coffee—$.78

Slab bacon—$.39 a pound
Hamburger—3 pounds for $1.00
Jell-O—3 packets for $.25
Kool-Aid—6 packets for $.25
Wheaties—2–12 oz. packages for $.43
Bananas—2 pounds for $.33
Big Jo Flour—50 lbs for $3.95

What a difference, he thought, between the huge Harlow Company, with its national advertising budget, and the little mercantile found only in Link Lake. What groceries his family bought they got from the Link Lake Mercantile. And his mother did buy Mother Harlow's Dills; after all, he worked for the Harlow Company.

He read the movie ads for the Palace Theater in Willow River. He had planned to take Amy to a movie one night when she was home, but that didn't happen. She would have enjoyed the current attraction, *Susan Slept Here,* with Dick Powell and Debbie Reynolds, or next week's show, *The Country Girl,* with Bing Crosby, Grace Kelly, and William Holden. But she had left on the train to Racine without as much as a good-bye to Andy.

He thought about how few people were going to movies these days, mostly only young people who were dating. Everyone else was watching television, staying up nights watching the flickering screen and talking about *I Love Lucy, The $64,000 Question,* and *The Ed Sullivan Show* the next day.

Andy put down the paper and headed out to the pickup. He thought about Amy and wondered how, after knowing her for so many years, growing up with her and attending elementary and high school with her, they could have developed such different perspectives about farming, about the future, and about life in general. Then he thought about his father and Amy's father: they saw the future of farming so differently it was unbelievable. It was obvious that Amy's ideas were her father's and her employer's. How wrong they were, Andy thought. If everyone believed as they did, there would be no more small family farms, no more cucumber patches, and no more people with close ties to the land. Farming would turn from growing food to producing a product. The land would no longer be something special but just another kind of factory. Inputs and outputs. Seed, fertilizer, and water in. Corn, cucumbers, potatoes, wheat, and oats out. The factory way. Measure the inputs. Measure the outputs. Farmer as factory worker, machine operator, and technician rather than steward, custodian, and caretaker. Andy thought, *And there's my girlfriend—she was my girlfriend—working at one of those damn factories.*

And now his father and Jake Stewart were rapidly becoming enemies over these same issues. Andy knew he wanted to be a farmer, but would there be a place for him? Could he farm as he wanted to farm, not as some university agriculturist or some pickle factory boss thought he should?

As he traveled the four miles to town, he passed by fields of ripening oats, and fields of corn, now taller than he was and tasseling. He saw pastures of cattle grazing, let out after the morning milking: Holsteins, Guernseys, and Jerseys, depending upon the farmer's preference. He drove by Otto Grableski's farm, where there were a few cows of each breed, even a couple cows of mixed heritage. Otto was not devoted to one kind of dairy cow, just as he cared not a whit about the tractor he drove. Some of his neighbors would argue to the point of fistfights over the virtues of John Deere or Farmall. Otto considered all this nonsense, but he said nothing. Farmers were entitled to their own opinions, no matter how diverse and unusual they might be.

Andy's morning drive was usually a pleasant one. He saw little traffic other than the milk hauler making his rounds with his big enclosed truck, stopping at each farm to lift the five or six and sometimes ten milk cans from the cooling tanks and hoist them on his truck, talking to the farmer if he happened to be nearby— a word about the weather, about the crops, about the price of milk these days.

But today Andy was weary. The summer cucumber season had been exceedingly good so far, but this meant long hours of sorting and salting, and short tempers and unruly help. Mostly it meant keeping his eye on Quarter Mile Sweet and Blackie Antonelli, who just didn't get along. Andy had thought that as the summer wore on they would learn to put up with each other. It hadn't happened. In fact, their bickering had gotten worse. Quarter Mile, who had been mild-mannered and quiet at the beginning of the season, had become as belligerent and mean as Blackie. The relationship between Helen Swanson and Preacher had gone in the other direction. They ate all their meals together, off by themselves, sometimes in the pickle factory office but often outside under a tree.

"What's going on between those two?" Blackie had asked Andy one day.

"It's because of her divorce," Andy answered. "She said she needs counseling and Preacher said he's had lots of counseling experience."

"Looks like more than counseling to me," Blackie said with a sneer in his voice. "Lots more going on than counseling."

"Blackie, they're both doing their jobs. If it gets to be a problem I'll take care of it."

Both were doing their jobs, better than ever, in fact. Helen was keeping track of all the records, writing all the checks, and figuring the salt for each day's intake of cucumbers. Preacher, who had been so frail and weak at the beginning of the season, tossed around bushel crates filled with cucumbers as well as the next worker. And he had learned to keep his mouth shut about religion. The crew had grown to like the guy, especially since the day he had stood between Blackie Antonelli and Jesús Moreno and had prevented what could have been a bloody, even deadly fight. But Preacher was still a mystery to his fellow workers. He worked hard, was polite, and never shirked his duties—in fact, he was usually one of the first to offer to help someone. One day Blackie had piled too many boxes of cucumbers on the cart and started pulling it over the rough plank floor to the cucumber vat in the far corner of the factory. It was Preacher who had run to prevent cucumbers from spilling all over the pickle factory floor and maybe falling on Blackie and injuring him. Andy had seen it from the office.

And, of course, not enough could be said about Agnes Swarsinski. Agnes with the eagle eye, Blackie said of her, Agnes who could spot a spoiled cucumber almost from the moment it was dumped from its gunnysack. Agnes always had a one-liner ("Never argue with an idiot. People watching can't tell the difference"), a little poem ("Roses are red, violets are blue, cucumbers are neither"), or a story ("the one about the . . .") that kept spirits high around the cucumber sorter on long afternoons that dragged into even longer evenings. Just the other day, Jake Stewart's migrants had brought in three truckloads of cucumbers and everyone had to sort well past midnight. Tempers were getting short that night as sack after sack was dumped on the sorter. Right in the middle of all of that, Agnes had said, "Pull the sorter switch." Andy thought that something had gotten caught in the sorter, maybe a stone or a stick—these sometimes showed up in the cucumber sacks. But there was no problem. Agnes had stopped the pickle sorting to tell a story. She began:

"There was this beech tree and a birch tree in the woods with a much smaller tree growin' between them. One day the two older trees were talkin' and wonderin' which of them was the father of the little tree. They decided to hire a pileated woodpecker to do some checkin'. The big woodpecker tapped on the beech tree, the red tuft on his head movin' up and down like a jackhammer. Then he tapped on the birch tree. Finally he tapped long and hard on the little tree. The two big trees were anxious for the results. The pileated woodpecker, red tuft shinin' in the bright sunlight and black wings tucked against its side, declared: 'The little tree is not a son of a beech. It is also not a son of a birch. But I must say, after tappin' on the little tree, that it was the best piece of ash I've had in a long time.'"

At first Andy was a little put out with what Agnes had done, because he knew there were lots of cucumbers to sort. The migrants had gone back to Jake Stewart's, leaving a huge pile of sacked cucumbers on the receiving floor. But Andy quickly saw what Agnes was doing. Not only did she have an eye for bad cucumbers, she had an eye for tempers that were about to flare and for workers who might start swinging at each other with the slightest provocation. Now everyone was laughing, something they had not done all day. Laughing out loud, surprised that a woman would tell such a tale. Even Preacher managed a smile.

Later, Agnes shared with Andy that she had seen Helen and Preacher kissing in back of the salt bin one noon. She thought Andy should know. "Sort of glad to see that the Preacher is human," Agnes offered.

"Guess he's a sinner like the rest of us," Andy replied, smiling.

J. W. Johnson stopped by about once a week to check on things. At first he had insisted they wash the factory floor at least once a day, until Andy convinced him that all the water pouring through the cracks in the floor to the area underneath created mold. Johnson finally agreed that a good sweeping would be sufficient.

Johnson reminded Andy several times to tell Blackie to cut his hair. Andy said, "He does his work. Long hair doesn't bother me. If you want his hair cut, you tell him." Blackie kept his long hair.

Johnson could find no fault with Helen's records. Compared to the other Harlow pickle factories, the Link Lake factory had the most error-free record of all. As the days passed, Johnson showed up less often.

From Andy's perspective everything was holding together, some days less well than others. They did manage, no matter the squabbles among the crew, to process each day's cucumber delivery. Ultimately that's what counted, especially from J. W. Johnson's perspective.

Things were going less well in Andy's personal life. Several days after Link Lake Pickle Days, Andy found a letter on the kitchen table when he returned home from the pickle factory. It was from Amy Stewart.

Dear Andy,

This will be short. I thought it only fair to tell you that I am going out with a fellow here at Case. He works in the tractor division.

I hope we can still be friends as we have been all these years. The best to you as you follow your dreams.

Your friend,
Amy

13

School Closing

The notice in the *Link Lake Gazette* stated simply, "All members of the Rose Hill School District are invited to a special meeting, August 11, 8 p.m. at the schoolhouse to discuss consolidation."

The meeting time allowed farmers to finish milking their cows, tote the cans of fresh milk to their milk houses and immerse them in cooling tanks, and turn their cows out to night pasture. Those who had a few sacks of cucumbers to deliver to the pickle factory did so in the late afternoon in anticipation of the evening meeting.

Most people in the Rose Hill School District were first- and second-generation immigrants, having come mostly from Germany and other northern European countries such as Norway, Poland, England, Ireland, and Wales. These people felt strongly about certain things, and the education of their children was one of them. They all agreed that schooling would help their children get ahead, no matter what they did with their lives.

Many dreaded school consolidation. It meant closing country schools and busing children to a village or city school. For these people, consolidation also meant rural communities lost considerable control of their children's education. And, most profoundly, consolidation meant that rural communities lost their identities, because these communities then took on the names of their school districts: Pleasant Valley, Willow Grove, Smith, Twin Oaks, High Bridge, Rose Hill.

Cars filled the schoolyard and were lined up on both sides of the road that ran past the building by the time Andy and his folks arrived. They found seats in the fast-filling schoolhouse. The big windows on the north and south sides of the building were open, but the room was hot and humid, like the weather outside. Not a whisper of a breeze on this mid-August night. A cicada was calling from one of the big oak trees next to the woodshed—its distinctive, raspy sound could be heard through the open schoolhouse windows. People also heard the distant rumble of thunder coming from the bank of dark clouds building in the west, behind the big woods that crowded up to the schoolyard fence on two sides.

"'Spect it'll rain tonight," a farmer said to the fellow next to him.

"Sure could use it. Cucumbers are startin' to wilt. Corn's startin' to fire on the bottom. Pasture's gettin' slim. Sure could use a good rain."

School board president Jake Stewart stood up. He was wearing a new pair of bib overalls. He walked from the back to the front of the room in his characteristic style, leaning forward. His big chin was jutting out, and he had his mouth set. The room was immediately quiet.

"You all know why we're here," he began in his high-pitched voice. Just hearing him talk made some people angry. "It's time we faced the future of the Rose Hill School," he said and then paused and looked around the room. He knew who his supporters were, and he also knew who opposed his idea of closing the school and busing the children to Link Lake. The school district was about evenly split between those in favor of closing the Rose Hill School and those who wanted to keep it open. His old friend, Isaac, firmly believed the school should remain open. But Isaac had decided it would be best to keep his feelings to himself during the meeting.

"We have a visitor from Madison who's been studying country schools and knows how to improve the education for our kids," Jake began. Sweat began trickling down his cheeks. He yanked an enormous red handkerchief from his pocket and ran it over his face, shook it, and stuffed it back in his pocket.

"This here is Dr. Julius Jensen. He's a professor and he's been studying country kids and how well they're learning," Jake said. "Let's give him a big Rose Hill School welcome." There was some polite clapping, like country folks will do when a politician they don't plan to vote for rolls into town and crawls up on a hay wagon and starts to talk.

Professor Jensen was a tall, thin fellow with a shock of white hair that fell over his eyes, causing him to regularly brush it back. He wore a white shirt and a blue bow tie that sagged to the right, more so as the evening progressed.

"It is my great pleasure to be here this evening," Professor Jensen began. "You are fortunate to have such a forward-looking school board president as Jake Stewart. Let's give him a round of applause for his leadership and, yes, for his vision." About half of the group clapped, immediately informing the good professor of what he was facing on this warm evening. The cicada had stopped, but the occasional rumble of thunder seemed louder to the room full of perspiring farmers and their families.

"I am a product of a one-room country school. I attended one for eight years in Minnesota," Jensen continued. "I know their good points, and, yes, I know about their shortcomings, too."

"You for closin' this school or not?" piped up Allan Clayton, one of Isaac Meyer's neighbors. Clayton was a man of few words and expected the same of others. He was sweating profusely.

"I'll be getting to that in just a few minutes," Professor Jensen answered.

"Well, you'd be savin' us a bunch of time if you'd get at it right now. It's hotter than hell in here, in case you haven't noticed," Clayton added, rubbing one arm distractedly.

There was some chuckling around the room, as the women were fanning themselves with whatever was handy and the men were swabbing their faces with red or blue handkerchiefs.

"Yes, you are certainly right about the heat. It's a warm evening."

Professor Jensen had a briefcase full of research findings, and come hell or high water, he was going to share the results. He leaned over and very deliberately pulled out a stack of papers and piled them on the teacher's desk that stood to his left.

"I have been researching rural schools for more than ten years," he continued. He once more pushed back a strand of hair. "And I've found some interesting things." He turned to the blackboard behind him and wrote across the top "Rural Schools" and "Consolidated Schools." Then to one side he listed, one on top of the other: "Reading," "Math," "Social Studies," "Science," "Language," "Physical Education."

"Do you know what the test scores show?" he asked. His bow tie had dipped farther to the right and now was at a forty-five-degree angle. His white shirt showed huge wet areas under each arm.

At this point in the meeting no one much cared about test scores; they wanted to debate closing or not closing the school. As the room got hotter, tempers grew shorter. The room was filled with human electricity; everyone could feel it. Thunder rumbled again in the west, and those sitting closest to the windows caught a glimpse of lightning cutting across the blackening sky.

Jensen put a plus sign next to each of the subjects under the consolidated school heading and a negative sign next to each item under the rural school category.

"We cannot argue with these data. They tell us clearly and without any question that our rural schools are failing."

"I don't know the meaning of your damn pluses and minuses. What about this school? You got numbers for this school?" Floyd Jenks piped up. "I wanna hear about this school, not about other schools."

"Let me explain how I did my research," Jensen said.

"Listen, Professor, I don't give a God damn about how you did your research. It all sounds like a bunch of bullshit to me," Jenks said. His face was red. Several people in the audience clapped loudly, an encouragement for Floyd Jenks to continue.

"You guys come out here from Madison and try to tell us how to run our school. You don't know diddly-squat about what goes on out here. We're a bunch of farmers trying to make a livin', trying to keep things goin'. We milk a few cows, grow some cucumbers, pay our taxes, and stay out of jail. What the hell gives you the right tellin' us our kids ain't learning what they're supposed to be learnin'? Tell me that. What the hell gives you the right?"

More clapping, even a loud whistle. Jake Stewart slowly got to his feet. Perspiration dripped from his brow.

"Let's be civil about this," he said in a voice that was even higher than usual. "What kind of impression is Professor Jensen gonna have of us with such talk?"

"Jake," Floyd Jenks said, now standing and looking his neighbor right in the eye. "I don't give a shit what he thinks. I don't give a shit what the entire damn University of Wisconsin thinks. They ain't but a bunch of overeducated bastards trying to tell us how we should lead our lives. A bunch of overeducated bastards." More clapping.

"We've had this school goin' for seventy-five years," Floyd continued. "My pa went to school here, I went to school here, and my kids go here now. By God, it was good enough for Pa, and it was good enough for me, and it's good enough for my kids. Let's all get the hell out of here and get on home 'fore the storm breaks."

"If I could have another moment," Professor Jensen said. He had removed his perspiration-soaked bow tie, unbuttoned his shirt at the neck, and rolled up his sleeves.

"As I said earlier, I attended a one-room school, as did my father and grandfather, and we got reasonably good educations. But the world is changing, and the one-room country schools can't provide what our children need for the future." Now it was time for the other side of the room to clap.

"Your children need more mathematics, more science with laboratory opportunities, more everything. You can't expect one teacher to handle all eight grades anymore. She just can't know everything that needs to be taught. It is humanly impossible." The rumble of thunder almost drowned out his last words.

"It is not 1900 anymore. Everything is changing, and quickly. How many of you have switched from horses to tractors? How many of you no longer milk cows by hand? How many of you still read by the light of a kerosene lamp? How many of you have a television set?" As the professor asked questions, people's hands went up. A few Rose Hill farmers still used horses on occasion, but almost all of them, with the exception of one or two, had tractors as well. Only one family in the school district did not have electricity, and these were the only people who did not raise their hands when asked if they had television sets.

The first gust of wind from the storm rattled the windows on the south side of the old building, and a welcome burst of cool air flowed into the room.

People began to listen to the professor. Most had their minds made up before they entered the building. They were either in favor of closing the school or they were not. But now most could not argue with the white-haired man at the front of the room. He continued, "Jonas Salk did the first tests of a polio vaccine just three years ago. And you all know about polio and the terrible toll it took on our young people." There were nods of agreement.

"To have more Jonas Salks, our children need the best possible mathematics and science educations they can get."

Floyd Jenks was listening to all this with one eye on the window and the approaching storm. He interrupted in a loud voice, "But our kids are gonna be farmers. They don't need a fancy education to work on a farm. In fact, they get too much learnin' and they'll leave for the cities."

Jensen thought he might be in trouble with his next line of argument, but he decided to pursue it anyway. He pushed back on his rolled-up sleeves. "We won't need as many farmers in the future. With new technology, one farmer can do the work of many. Our rural young people will need to find jobs off the farm, and for that they need the best education they can get."

He barely got the last words out of his mouth when the room nearly erupted. No matter what their position on closing the Rose Hill School, the idea of their children having to leave the farm just didn't go down right, like trying to swallow blood sausage when you couldn't stomach the idea of how it was made.

A brilliant flash of lightning and an almost simultaneous clap of thunder shook the old building. Lightning had struck one of the big oak trees just beyond the pump house, but many in the room thought it had hit the school. Two women screamed. Several children began crying. The lights blinked twice and then went out, throwing the room into total darkness. A driving rain began sifting through the open windows as the angry crowd tried to find the door in the dark.

Jake Stewart found a kitchen match in his pocket and struck it against a school desk. The dim flickering light was enough for people to find the door and move down the schoolhouse steps in search of their cars. The rain came off the schoolhouse roof in torrents. As people hurried, they turned to look back, to see if the schoolhouse had been struck by lightning. But it stood straight and tall, as it had for seventy-five years. A good number hoped it would stand straight and tall for another seventy-five.

Professor Jensen was left standing alone on the front steps of the old schoolhouse, in the rain and dark.

14

Salt Bin

With the soaking rain, no cucumbers could be picked the following morning. The crew at the pickle factory needed a break. But there was no time for relaxation. Helen needed to keep the records up-to-date, the cucumber sorter required cleaning and oiling, several wooden cucumber boxes had loose slats and needed renailing, and broken boards covering the pickle vats called for repair. But the big job for the day was emptying a boxcar-load of salt that had arrived sometime in the night, when the Chicago and Northwestern Railroad's northbound freight had unhooked the car and located it on the railroad's pickle factory siding.

Andy noticed the salt car when he arrived at the factory—he had been expecting it but hadn't known the exact date it would come. He pulled open the boxcar door to see salt, tons of it, piled about four feet high. A wooden gate prevented the loose salt from tumbling out when the car door was pulled open.

Andy considered which workers he should ask to shovel salt— the procedure required two men standing in the car, shoveling salt onto an electric-powered canvas conveyor belt that moved the material from the railcar to the salt bin. A third person worked in the bin, shoveling the salt around so it filled uniformly. All three jobs were backbreaking, miserable work. The inside of the car was stifling hot, and it was even warmer in the windowless salt bin.

Helen Swanson arrived shortly after Andy, all smiles and bubbly.

"Hi there, Andy," she said as she walked into the office. For the first time in many months she felt like her old self, thanks to Preacher's skilled counseling and personal attention. Talk around the pickle factory about the two of them didn't bother her. But she was a little miffed hearing the rumors spreading to downtown Link Lake where a bunch of busybody old women were always looking for juicy gossip. It was none of their business.

Helen snapped on the little Philco radio that stood on her desk, and the factory filled with the sounds of hit songs that Helen enjoyed: "Unchained Melody," "Cherry Pink and Apple Blossom White," "Earth Angel," "You My Love" sung by Frank Sinatra, Doris Day doing "Love Me or Leave Me."

Preacher arrived next. He stuck his head in the office door, said hi to Helen, and then asked Andy what he should do.

"Why don't you start cleaning the sorter," Andy said. "Scrape the crud off the sorter bars first; farmers are complaining they aren't getting many number-one cucumbers these days. They may be right. With all the dirt on the sorter bars, it takes a smaller cucumber to make number one. Got to fix that, or Johnson will be on me. Got a carload of salt to unload, too. May ask you to help with that once Quarter Mile and Blackie get here."

Agnes slowly climbed the steps to the factory floor and then walked over to where Andy and Preacher worked at the sorter.

"Good mornin'," she said as a big smile spread across her face. "Say, do you know what happens when two bullets marry?"

"No, what happens when two bullets marry?" Andy responded with a smile.

"They have a BB."

Andy and Preacher both rolled their eyes.

"Hey, what's up this mornin'? Kinda wet for pickin' cukes, ain't it?"

"How about helping Preacher clean up the sorter until the other two get here. Got salt to unload today, and it feels like it's gonna be a hot muggy one. No fun shoveling salt on a day like this, but we gotta do it. Almost out of salt."

Quarter Mile Sweet and Blackie Antonelli arrived at the same time, parking their cars under the big shade trees west of the pickle factory. They did not so much as acknowledge each other's existence as they climbed the factory steps side by side.

"What do we do today?" Blackie asked Andy. "Doubt we'll see many cukes until this afternoon."

"Salt car came in last night. I want you and Quarter Mile to unload it. Preacher here will work in the salt bin. You can take your time, but we gotta have it unloaded before we leave tonight."

Blackie had helped unload the car in other years, so he knew where to find the conveyor and how to set it up with one end in the boxcar and the other in the salt bin. Soon salt was spilling off the end of the conveyor into the salt bin, where Preacher was shoveling it into the corners.

Quarter Mile and Blackie, both stripped to their waists, were soon dripping sweat as they stood ankle-deep in the salt, one on each side of the conveyor, taking turns shoveling salt onto the canvas belt. They tried to ignore each other.

They had worked for about an hour when it happened. Andy later tried to piece together how the fight had started, but as is usually the case with these kinds of altercations, it depended on whom you asked. Blackie said that Quarter Mile started the fight, and Quarter Mile said it was Blackie who threw a shovel full of salt on him and started it all.

Around eleven o'clock Andy heard loud words coming from the salt car. "You sonofabitch," Quarter Mile yelled in a voice that could be heard at the sawmill a couple hundred yards away.

"You college bastard," Blackie said in an equally loud voice.

Andy rushed to the salt car. He quickly noticed that no more salt was moving up the conveyor belt. Blackie sat astride Quarter Mile, pounding him in the face. Then Quarter Mile struck Blackie in the nose, and blood squirted out like a faucet had opened. It quickly soaked into the salt, leaving a red stain on the white surface.

"What in hell you guys doing?" Andy said as he peered through the door of the boxcar.

Agnes and Preacher rushed over to the salt bin, followed quickly by Helen.

The young men staggered to their feet. Blood continued streaming from Blackie's nose.

"The bastard busted my nose," Blackie said, putting his hand to his face. "God damn you, Quarter Mile, you busted my nose." Blackie's long hair was so covered with salt that it looked white.

Quarter Mile gasped for breath, his sides heaving. Blood streamed from a cut above his right eye, nearly blinding him. The incredible pain of salt in the cuts was evident in his expression.

"This damn dago sonofabitch threw salt on me," he blurted out. At those words, Blackie took a huge swing at Quarter Mile and missed, falling into the salt. Immediately Quarter Mile was on top of him.

Once again they rolled in the salt, pounding each other unmercifully.

"Stop it!" Andy yelled. But it was like talking to the wind.

"Blessed are the peacemakers," Preacher said reverently.

"Quit your damn fighting!" Andy yelled again. But there was no response from the two young men, both bleeding profusely.

"I'm bettin' my money on Quarter Mile," Agnes said. "Anybody put any money on Blackie?"

"Betting is a sin," said Preacher

"You're not helping things, Agnes," Andy said.

"Could see this comin'," Agnes said.

"This is not something for you to see, Helen," Preacher said, motioning for her to return to the office. Helen ignored him.

Andy rolled the boxcar door shut and let the two young men have at it. It was the only thing he could think to do.

"Maybe this will clear the air," Agnes said, seeming to agree with Andy's action.

"Violence solves nothing," Preacher said, looking at Agnes.

With the door shut, for a few minutes only muffled yells could be heard from inside; then it was quiet.

Andy yanked open the door. Blackie lay half-buried in the salt, blood streaming from his broken nose and from several other cuts on his face. Quarter Mile, also bleeding profusely from cuts above both eyes, stood over him, glaring. His sweaty body was covered with salt.

"Guess I bet right, brains over brawn every time. I'll get the water hose," Agnes said, not waiting for a response to her comment.

Andy and Preacher dragged Blackie to his feet and helped him from the salt car. With the hose, Agnes washed the salt and gore from Blackie. Then she cleaned off Quarter Mile. He didn't look the worse for the fight, except for his right eye, which was rapidly swelling shut.

"Better get Blackie to a doctor," Preacher said. Helen volunteered to drive him to the Link Lake Clinic.

Andy now faced three problems. The car was only half-unloaded. He had to write a report to J. W. Johnson about Blackie's injuries. And he was quite sure he'd have to hire a short-term replacement for Blackie. The first problem he solved by ordering Quarter Mile Sweet back into the salt car, bruised and battered as he was, and scarcely able to see out of one eye. Andy joined Quarter Mile shoveling salt, something he hadn't done since the first year he was manager. After a few minutes, he once more discovered how miserable the job was.

As much as Quarter Mile must have hurt and however much his wounds stung with all the salt in them, he shoveled all afternoon without complaint. Thankfully, the first load of cucumbers did not arrive until after supper, so Andy and Quarter Mile were able to shovel without interruption.

Andy and Quarter Mile were still shoveling salt when Blackie and Helen returned from the clinic. Blackie got into his car and left, not even coming inside the pickle factory. Helen told Andy that Blackie had a broken finger along with a broken nose, and that the doctor had ordered him to take a few days off work.

Andy asked Helen to fill out an accident report stating that Blackie Antonelli had been injured while shoveling salt—it was the truth. J. W. Johnson didn't need to know the details of the matter, although he would probably ask how a worker could receive a broken nose while shoveling. Andy decided to tell Johnson, if he asked, that Blackie had slipped and fallen on the conveyor belt. When he told his plan to Helen, she raised an eyebrow.

"Well, it could have happened that way," Andy said.

"Sure," Helen said, smiling. "But I won't tell."

Now Andy knew he would need to replace Blackie for a few days. The crew couldn't handle several truckloads of cucumbers; three loads from Jake Stewart's thirty-acre cucumber field would roll in that night alone.

George Roberts had worked at the pickle factory a year ago but had gone off on a drinking binge and hadn't shown up for three days. Andy had called his home and told him not to bother showing up for work again, and he hadn't. Roberts had applied again this season, but Andy hadn't called him.

When he wasn't drinking, Roberts was a good worker. He was fifty years old and had worked for twenty-five years at the sawmill. They fired him when he came to work drunk one day. A sawmill was dangerous enough when everyone was sober— drinking could not be condoned.

The pickle factory had its dangers, too, but nothing compared to a sawmill.

Now Andy had his back against the wall. He called George. "It's Andy Meyer over at the pickle factory," he said when George answered the phone. "How you feeling?"

"Feelin' good, Andy. Feelin' good." George replied. When George was drinking, he was one mouthful of complaints— everything about him hurt, it seemed.

"Took the cure over in Oshkosh last month. Took the cure, Andy. No more boozin'. Cold sober I am these days, Andy. Cold sober."

"You like to work over here at the pickle factory for a few days? One of the men got hurt and is home recuperating."

"What time you want me, Andy? I'll come whenever you say. Come whenever you say."

"How about tomorrow morning at eight?"

"I'll be there Andy. Be there with bells on, Andy. Yesiree."

Shorthanded, it took the pickle factory crew until well past midnight to complete the sorting and salting. By the time he left for home, Quarter Mile's right eye was completely swollen shut. Andy wondered what he would tell his mother; he expected a call from her—and he decided to tell her the truth about what happened.

When he got home that evening, he learned from his folks that their longtime neighbor Allan Clayton had died of a massive heart attack. It had not been a good day.

15

George Roberts

As he had promised, George Roberts reported at the pickle factory promptly at eight the next day. Andy was waiting for him, hoping he was sober. "Well, I'm here, Andy. Here, just like I said I would be." George had a three-day growth of mostly gray whiskers that gathered in clumps around his jaw line. As they shook hands, Andy took his breath—and smelled cigarettes, but no alcohol. He remembered that George was a heavy smoker.

"Remember, George, no drinking, and no smoking in the building. You got to smoke outside."

"I got it, Andy," he said as he touched his long, thin finger to the side of his head. "Got it right here. Remember from last time I worked here. Remember about the smoking. Yup, I remember that. Remember that good. Old mind is still there, Andy. Brain still works."

"Want you to work on the sorter with Agnes. You remember Agnes, don't you?" Agnes Swarsinski was scraping dirt off the wooden sorter bars.

"Hey there, George," she said. "How the hell are ya?"

"I'm good Agnes. Feelin' good. Took the cure, you know. Over at Oshkosh."

"Hope it works out for you, George."

"Workin' out fine, Agnes. Workin' out fine so far. Things are comin' back together. Comin' back together for me."

"Meet Quarter Mile Sweet, George. He's new this year," Andy said.

"Jeez, what the hell happened to your eye?"

"Got into a little misunderstanding," Quarter Mile said.

"How'd the other fellow look?" George asked, grinning. He didn't put two and two together and figure out the reason he had a job might be because of a fight that Quarter Mile had been in.

"This is Preacher," Andy said. "He's also new here this year. Preacher's the pastor over at the Church of the Holy Redeemed."

"Well, I'm sure pleased to meet a man of the cloth. Sure pleased." George shook the preacher's hand. "'Spect you're keepin' down the swearin' around this place. Sure as hell been a problem durin' past summers. Sure has."

"So pleased the Lord has saved you from the devil's drink," Preacher said.

"Yup, he sure as hell did," George replied, smiling.

"Let's go see Helen," Andy said. "Get your payroll stuff straight. Got your Social Security card with you?"

"Nope, but I know the number. Got it right up here, Andy." Once more he tapped on the side of his head.

"How are you, George?" Helen asked by way of a greeting.

"Doin' fine, Helen. Doin' fine. Things gettin' better. Gettin' better everyday. How about you, Helen? How you doin'? Heard you've had some tough sleddin'. Tough sleddin' without a man around. Woman needs a man." Helen rolled her eyes.

"Here, fill this out," she said, handing a piece of paper and a pencil to George.

"Yup, I'll fill 'er out, fill 'er out right now." George sat down at the side of the desk and scratched some basic information about himself on the standard H. H. Harlow employment form.

"What do I write on this line, Helen? Asks about my last permanent job and why I left. What do I say here? Reason was I was drunk and they fired me. Do I write that down? Don't sound right to put that down. I ain't drunk now. Ain't drunk now, am I, Helen?"

"No, you don't appear to be." Helen smiled when she said it.

"Well, I ain't. I took the cure over at Oshkosh. Place where they help guys like me give up drinkin'. You know about the cure over at Oshkosh, Helen?"

"I've heard of it."

"You don't ever want to go there. Helluva place for a human being. One helluva place. But it works, Helen. You quit drinkin'."

Looking at George's employment file, Helen suggested, "Why don't you just write, 'Left employment at Link Lake Sawmill after twenty-five years.'"

"I'll do that, Helen. That's what I'll write. Won't be lying, will I, Helen?"

"No, you won't be lying, George."

George slowly wrote the words on the employment form.

"Well, here she is, Helen. All filled out like you wanted. Even remembered to sign my John Henry on the bottom. Signed it right there, place where it says to sign."

"Hope things get better for you, George," Helen said. She knew George's reputation around Link Lake.

"Things gettin' better, Helen. Better every day. Just you watch

now, I'm a changed person, Helen. No more heavy drinkin'."
George said.

"Well, welcome back to the pickle factory."

"Thank you, Helen. Needed this job. Sure as hell needed this
job. Bitch just sittin' around doin' nothin'. Nobody wantin' to
hire you, nobody even givin' you the time of day. Not even givin'
you the time of day. Like you weren't there or something. Know
how that is, Helen? When people look right past you? People you
knew all your life. Look right past you, Helen. Like you was the
scum of the earth. It's a bitch when people do that."

"Happens to divorced women, too," Helen said. "Some of
your old friends will cross the street just so they don't have to say
hello."

"Bitch when that happens, Helen. A bitch. Don't know why
people do that. Why do they get so high and mighty? Like they
ain't never did anything wrong. Everbody's done somethin' wrong.
You bet they have. You just don't know about it 'cause they know
how to hide their bad ways. People know how to hide their faults,
Helen."

"You better get to work, George."

"Yeah, I'd better. Good talkin' with you. You just keep your
chin up, Helen. Keep your chin up."

"I'll do that, George." In the background the radio was quietly
playing "Love Is a Many-Splendored Thing," the Four Aces' popular tune.

As he left the office, George mumbled, "Yup, that love is a
splendid thing."

The first load of cucumbers, a pickup truck with a half-dozen
sacks, had pulled up to the unloading dock.

"Let me help you unload those," George said, leaning over to grab one of the sacks Bill Steinke, a farmer from east of town, handed up to him. He pulled the full gunnysack of cucumbers in front of the sorter. "Cukes got a lot heavier since last I worked here," George said. He leaned over and grabbed another sack as it was pushed up to him.

"You got rocks in this sack?" George asked, smiling. "Seems like there's more than cukes in this one."

"Only cucumbers, George." Steinke recognized George. In fact, nearly everyone around Link Lake knew George Roberts and his drinking problem. They also knew that he could never keep a job these days, even though he was a good worker. He'd work hard for a week or so and then go off on a drinking binge and get fired.

"By the way, how you doin' George? You feelin' better?"

"Feelin' better. Feelin' better everyday." George had seen Steinke in town before but didn't remember his name. "Took the cure over in Oshkosh."

"Good for you, George."

"Yup, took the cure. Off the bottle. Old self is comin' back."

Steinke walked up the steps and over to the scale, where Andy was waiting to weigh the cucumbers coming off the sorter. The two men talked quietly about the usual topics: the weather, the good harvest, the price of cukes. George untied the first sack, lifted the cucumbers up to the sorter, and dumped them in. He hadn't done any physical work for several months, and his knees wobbled under the weight. He repeated this with the second sack and then waited as the cucumbers shook their way across the sorting bars under Agnes's careful eye.

"You know what was best about the cure over in Oshkosh?" George said to Agnes.

"Can't imagine," Agnes replied, not looking up from the sea of green cucumbers that moved in front of her.

"When it was over. That was the best part of that whole damn experience. Best part, Agnes."

"Sometimes works that way."

"Know what I did to celebrate when it was over?"

"What was that, George?"

"We stopped in Omro on the way home."

"That's a nice town."

"You bet it is. I was lookin' for a saloon."

"Thought you took the cure."

"Did take the cure. Took the cure."

"Why you stoppin' at a saloon on the way home, then?"

"Needed to celebrate a little. Needed a couple of stiff drinks. Only a couple. That's all I had. Only a couple stiff ones. No where's near enough to get drunk. Just a couple drinks."

"Sounds like you didn't quit drinkin', George."

"Didn't quit all the way. Who'd wanna do that? Maybe some Baptist. Some Baptist might wanna do that. But guess they don't start drinkin' in the first place. Heard that about some Baptists. Heard they never take a drink. Not one. Not ever. Can't imagine what that'd be like. Can you imagine that, Agnes?"

"Hey, quit talkin' and dump in another sack of cukes."

"Yeah, here they come. Here comes more cucumbers." George dumped the next two sacks.

"You know about Baptists, Agnes?"

16

Ames County Fair

Everyone in Ames County attended the fair. Old timers remembered when the draft horse judging was the major event. Kids in 4-H exhibited calves and cooking and sewing and woodworking projects such as doorstops and chick feeders. Kids too young for 4-H mostly came to ride the Tilt-a-Whirl that jerked them around in a circle and the Loop-de-Loop that turned them upside down and dumped their loose change on the ground. Those with five dollars could take an airplane ride in a big double-wing, open-cockpit plane where the pilot sat in the back and the passenger in front.

"Fly you over your farm," the pilot said as he leaned on a wing, a cigarette hanging out of his mouth. "See what your place looks like from a crow's-eye view."

Many people attended the fair for the carnival, featuring games of chance (knock over the milk bottles!), rides like the Ferris Wheel and Merry-Go-Round, and food tents (offering everything from cotton candy to hamburgers with onions).

Farmers came to see the lineup of machinery, the new tractors—Allis Chalmers orange, Oliver green, International red,

John Deere green and yellow, Massey-Harris red. In those days huge arguments arose over which was better, red or green—with the focus on John Deere and International. The other tractor makes were minor players, present but not important in any major debate.

Farmers climbed on tractor seats, kicked tires, inspected engines, asked the dealer to start them up as they stood watching, listening, and wishing they had the money to buy one of these shiny new machines.

These men and their sons, sometimes with wives and daughters, too, walked by the new grain combines that would cut and thresh the grain as the machine rolled across the field. It would replace the threshing machine that made the rounds about this time every year, in mid-August. They peered into the machine, asked how it worked, looked at the price, and then shook their heads.

"Don't think we'd want one of them. What'd happen to the threshing crews if everybody had a combine? Besides, who can afford one?" someone asked.

"Threshing machines are a thing of the past," the dealer standing nearby said. "Thing of the past. Most of the farmers in the southern part of the state, in Dane and Rock and Walworth Counties, have already switched to combines. These farmers swear by them. Say they'll never go back to threshing. Too much work. Combines make harvesting grain a lot easier."

"Well, this ain't the southern part of the state," a grizzled old farmer said, sending a stream of tobacco juice to the ground just to the right of the salesman's shoes. The salesman jumped a little to the side.

"You almost got me," the salesman said jovially.

"Guess I did at that. Aim's a little off these days," the farmer said.

"Here, take one of these folders along with you," he said, not letting up on his sales pitch.

The farmer took the colorful folder and walked away, brushing his big calloused hand across his chin and grinning from ear to ear. He tossed the folder in the nearest trash barrel.

The fair opened at the Willow River fairgrounds the third week in August, and the *Link Lake Gazette* had begun reporting fair-related events weeks earlier. A big supporter of the fair, the paper also included highlights of the previous year's fair—who had won the cow calling contest, who exhibited the grand champion cucumber entry, and details about other important events that drew people to the fairgrounds each year.

The fair started on Thursday, with exhibitors hauling in their entries: cattle, vegetables, field crops, artwork, carpentry projects, paintings, photography, canned fruits, baked bread, cakes, pies, chickens (laying hens, broilers, roasters, and of course roosters, which crowed regularly), geese that began honking with first light of the morning, ducks, hogs, sheep, and horses (both saddle and draft types, although the draft horse numbers were dwindling each year as tractors took over farm work).

Except for this partial week in August, the fairgrounds nearly stood empty. County snowplows were stored in the buildings. The community celebrated the Fourth of July and Labor Day at the fairgrounds. But mostly the place was abandoned, except during the fair, when the place came to life. The sounds and smells of the country were concentrated on a few acres on the south side of Willow River, where the city gave way to farmland.

The fairgrounds took up about thirty acres. A woven wire fence surrounded the grounds, to keep out those who wanted to bypass the fifty-cent admission. Visitors to the fair first saw the ticket booth. From there, depending on their interests, they could stroll past the hog, sheep, and horse pens and walk through the two-story cattle barn—some of the 4-H members slept in the second story—or the fowl shed just beyond the cattle barn.

Members of 4-H clubs exhibited their woodworking, electricity, forestry, and other projects in a little building next to the cattle barn, and just beyond that was a large building that contained crop exhibits and vegetable exhibits—everything from corn and oats to cucumbers. Next came the "women's building"—where sewing, cooking, baking, canning, and knitting projects were displayed.

Most exhibits were judged on Friday and Saturday, but cucumber judging took place on Sunday afternoon, when the fair crowd reached its peak. For years the Link Lake Pickle Factory had shut down on Sunday afternoon so the employees could attend the fair and so the farmers could plan their cucumber picking around the fair schedule.

Andy Meyer rolled the factory doors shut precisely at noon on Sunday and set off for Willow River. The rest of the crew also headed to the fair. The competition for best cucumbers at the Ames County Fair was stiff—even tighter than at Link Lake Pickle Days. At the county fair, Ames County growers competed with cucumber growers from Portage, Waupaca, Adams, and Marquette counties. It was a high honor for a farmer to receive the grand champion ribbon (fondly known as the cucumber crown). The award winner received headlines in the *Link Lake Gazette* as well as in the *Milwaukee Journal* and the *Milwaukee Sentinel.* Last year Jake Stewart had won the coveted award, and he fully expected to win again. After all, he had thirty acres of cucumbers to select from.

When Andy arrived at the fairgrounds, he walked directly to the horticulture building, where a table the entire length of the building was green with cucumber entries. The judging was scheduled to begin at 2:00 p.m., and already people were sitting in the folding metal chairs set out for those who wanted to watch the event.

Andy found his pa's entry—it looked as good as any of the cucumbers, perhaps better than most. At one end of the table, Jake Stewart's entry had a prominent place, eight of the most beautiful cucumbers Andy had ever seen. The competition would once more be keen, and he was happy that he wasn't the judge.

The annual cow-calling contest was scheduled for one o'clock. An area near the cattle barn had been roped off for the event. Each contestant, male or female, young or old, would step up to a line, and then use his or her best cow-calling voice to lure a Jersey cow standing in a temporary pen at the far end of the roped-off area. The closer the cow came to the caller, the more points he or she got. The winner took home a trophy—a replica of a Jersey cow's head with her ears forward. It sounded easy enough, and many of the contestants were seasoned cow callers who used their calls to fetch their cattle from the night pastures every morning.

As he approached, Andy heard the judge explaining the rules. The first contestant stood at the line, a young woman who appeared not to have spent one day on a farm. She didn't even have a tan, so she obviously spent no time in a farm field hoeing, picking cucumbers, or doing much of anything else outside. But she was a big girl, tall and husky, and likely had a voice for cow calling even if she didn't have the experience.

"You ready?" the judge, a farmer from Marquette County, asked her.

"Yeah, I'm ready," she replied.

"Remember, you get three tries. Call away when you're ready."

The young woman took a deep breath, stood up straight, and looked off toward the Jersey cow, which was eating hay, oblivious to the entire goings on.

"Come cow," she yelled in a voice that caused those standing near her to jump back. "Come cow," she yelled again. The little Jersey lifted its head and looked in the direction of the noise.

"Come cow," the young woman yelled a third time; people in the nearby buildings could hear her.

The cow, unimpressed, turned back to eating hay.

"Let's have a round of applause for a good try," the judge said, his finger digging at his ear. "You got the volume, young lady, I'll hand you that. Three points for volume. Who's next?"

The next contestant was clearly a farmer. He wore bib overalls and a cap with John Deere emblazoned on the front.

"You ready?" the judge asked.

"I'm ready," the farmer said.

"Sueee, sueee," he yelled in a high-pitched voice. A few people in the crowd giggled, some laughed right out loud. Nobody had heard such a cow call before, mostly because it was a typical hog call.

"Sueee, sueee," the farmer called again, this time slightly louder. The Jersey looked up and took a couple steps toward the farmer making the strange noise. She seemed more curious than anything else. Evidently the little cow hadn't heard this call before, either.

"Sueee, sueee," the farmer called a third time. The Jersey turned and walked back to her pile of hay.

"Well, that's some call," the judge said, smiling.

"Yup, been doin' it for years. I only got hogs on my place, and when I let loose with that call they come a trottin'. Yes, they do."

"Well, this here is a cow you're calling today."

"I know that. Figured what'd bring hogs runnin' would do the same for a cow. Guess I was wrong."

"Two points for an interesting try," the judge said. "Next?"

Another farmer, a short man with an ample middle, took his place at the line.

"Dexter Applebee's my name," the fellow said, extending his hand to the judge. "This where I'm supposed to stand?"

"Yup, and you can start callin' anytime you're ready."

The little man stood up to his full five feet four or so, pushed back his shoulders, and lifted up his head.

"Ka-boss," he said in a loud, clear voice that drifted over the crowd kind of free and easy. The little Jersey quit eating hay and lifted her head.

"Ka-boss," he called again. The sound had a kind of melody to it, sort of musical, especially the way he drew out the boss part.

"Ka-boss," he called a third time. This time the Jersey walked out of the pen and began slowly walking toward the man, ignoring the crowd. She came within ten feet of him before she stopped and stood looking, her big brown eyes open wide and her ears standing forward. Then she turned and walked back to the little pile of hay that continued to draw her attention.

"Mighty good showing," the judge said. "Looks like we might have a winner here. Give you twenty points for that good try."

"Thank you," Dexter Appleby said, making a small bow to the crowd. "Thank you very much." The crowd cheered and clapped, thinking they had just seen the winning performance.

"Any more contestants?" the judge asked, looking over the crowd. A fellow in the back shuffled forward, a tall, thin farmer, who wore a straw hat, pants that were too short, and a shirt with sleeves that ended well before his hands began.

He took his place at the line. The Jersey cow looked up before he even opened his mouth.

"You ready?"

"I am," the fellow replied.

"Then give it a go."

"Ka-boss, ka-boss, ka-boss," the lanky farmer called in a rather soft voice. The little Jersey immediately began trotting toward him and didn't stop until she stood right in front of him. The farmer scratched her head and she nuzzled his shirt. He didn't bother to call the second or third time.

"Guess this here is our winner," the judge said. "Never seen a cow come so fast to a call. What's your name, fella?"

"Name is Charlie Corkhill."

"Where you from, Charlie?"

"Over by Pine River, not too far from Poy Sippi."

"Well, you get the prize this year. Newspaperman over there will want to talk to you, find out how you got to be such an effective cow caller."

"Much obliged for the award," Charlie said. "Much obliged."

After the fair was over, someone discovered that the little Jersey cow had been part of the Corkhill Jersey exhibit and belonged to Charlie himself. A bunch of people made quite a fuss about it and insisted that Dexter Appleby was the true winner and that Corkhill should give up the trophy because of fraud. Corkhill said he didn't know what that word, *fraud,* meant, and he wasn't about to give up his trophy. And that's how the matter stood. Another fair would come along in another year with another cow-calling contest. Somebody would make sure that a cow's owner wasn't allowed to compete in the Ames County Cow-Calling Contest, and the 1955 contest would be forgotten, by most folks, anyway.

After the cow-calling contest, Andy Meyer hurried back to the horticulture building. It was a few minutes past two, and the cucumber judging should be taking place. He heard a commotion well before he got to the building. He pushed his way inside—a huge crowd had gathered to watch the judging and to see the cucumber king crowned.

Near where the judging was taking place, Andy saw a very red-faced and perspiring Jake Stewart standing toe-to-toe with the cucumber judge, Michael Lauer. Lauer was the agricultural agent from Portage County and had judged cucumbers at the Ames County Fair for as long as anyone remembered. In his early fifties and rather rotund, wearing a felt hat, Lauer was standing his ground against this increasingly angry cucumber grower.

Andy saw his dad in the crowd and walked over to him.

"What's going on, Pa?" Andy asked.

"Judge just threw out Jake's entry. Said his cucumbers are diseased."

Jake Stewart yelled, "What do you mean, my cucumbers are disqualified?"

"I disqualify any diseased vegetable, and your cucumbers are diseased," the county agent said in a quiet voice.

"The hell they are," Jake yelled. "What's diseased about these cukes? Here, look. Look at them. They are perfect. Perfect cucumbers."

"They are diseased, Mr. Stewart," the agent replied, not backing down.

"Well, what disease they got?" Stewart asked. His voice was not quite as loud. The crowd around the two men had grown larger; even some of the women from the Lutheran Ladies Aid food stand had heard the ruckus and had come into the horticulture building. So had the John Deere dealer and the International dealer, both of whom had machinery displays just outside the building.

"Your cucumbers have spot rot," the agent said quietly.

"What in hell is spot rot?" Stewart asked. He was looking at his cucumbers, holding them as one would handle a prized possession.

Isaac Meyer eased near his old neighbor. "Calm down, Jake. No help in yelling."

"Hear what this bastard judge did?" Jake said, in a quieter voice.

"I heard, but let's listen to what he has to say."

The judge was talking to the entire group. "Spot rot starts with a tiny little spot, and then it invades the entire cucumber. Here, let me show you." The county agent picked up one of Jake's cucumbers and pointed to a tiny, grayish spot.

"See this?" the county agent said.

"Piece of dirt. Little piece of dirt," Jake said.

"Nope, not a piece of dirt. It's a little rotten spot."

"Son of a bitch," Jake said. "Son . . . of . . . a . . . bitch." He let the words drag out. "Do you have to tell everybody?" he said to the county agent.

"I want people to see what this is. It's serious," the county agent said.

"Well, I don't wanna hear any more." Jake whirled and stomped out of the building.

The county agent then turned to the crowd and began explaining more about spot rot. He said that in some parts of the Midwest, especially in Michigan, it had infected entire cucumber fields and shut down pickle factories.

"It's a terrible disease. Let's hope that Mr. Stewart's is only an isolated case. The disease spreads fast, and there is no cure for it."

Andy and Isaac Meyer listened carefully to what the county agent was saying. He offered some practical and sober advice. Andy looked closely at the spot rot on Jake Stewart's cucumbers so he could tell Agnes what he had learned the first thing tomorrow.

Outside the building, Andy said to his dad, "Sounds like serious stuff. Suppose we got any spot rot in our cucumber patch?"

"I'll look the first thing I get home," Isaac said. "Never heard of anything like this. If it spreads, what'll it do to the pickle factory?"

"That's just what I'm worried about. We're gonna have to inspect every cucumber we take in."

17

Disaster

The first thing Andy did on the Monday morning after the fair was talk to the factory crew about spot rot and what he had seen and heard the previous day. He said that Jake Stewart's entry at the fair was infected. It was a sobering moment. Everyone listened carefully to Andy's description of what to look for in a cucumber infected with spot rot.

"If spot rot gets a foothold here it could wipe out the rest of our season," Andy said. "But apparently it doesn't hit every cucumber patch. It misses some smaller ones entirely, according to the county agent who judged cucumbers at the fair. But once the disease gets here, nothing can stop it. About the only thing a farmer can do is deep plow the old vines and rotten cucumbers and find a new field for the next year."

"Terrible-sounding disease," Agnes said.

"Yeah, could be a disaster," Andy replied. "County agent said that the ag college in Madison is working on some new cucumber varieties that are resistant to the disease. But that doesn't help us this year."

"It'll be okay," Agnes said. "I'll look for the spots and toss out the bad cukes. We'll make it work."

Disaster

The first load of cucumbers arrived around nine that morning, and everyone was on the sorter except Helen, who was working in the office. Every cucumber was turned over, looked at, inspected. It took twice as long as usual to sort, but Andy wanted to make sure the cucumbers they bought were spot-rot free. This batch was clean, and so were the next five loads that arrived.

Andy hoped what he had seen at the county fair was an isolated incident. Maybe Jake Stewart had happened onto a few diseased cucumbers and the rest of his fields were disease-free. Maybe that's all it was—an isolated incident. Carlos Rodríguez's truck usually brought in the first load of Jake Stewart's cucumbers around three every afternoon and the second load right after supper. Andy wished his crew wouldn't find any problems with the Stewart cucumbers.

The factory crew had become a well-oiled group by this time in the cucumber season. Things were going smoothly, maybe because Blackie was still off work. Even George Roberts had stayed on the wagon, coming to work on time every day and apparently leaving his bottle on the shelf. And Agnes was her usual self, telling tall tales, spitting out witticisms, and keeping everyone entertained.

Just the other day, right out of the blue, she had said, "Better to keep your mouth shut and thought a fool than to start talking and remove all doubt."

"Huh?" Quarter Mile Sweet had said. He hadn't been listening. The hum and clatter of the cucumber sorter prevented easy conversation.

"I said, better to keep your mouth shut and thought a fool than to start talking and remove any doubt."

"You telling me that?" Quarter Mile said.

"Nope, just saying it for anybody who wants to hear," Agnes said, smiling. "It's a good rule, you know."

"If you say so, Agnes." Quarter Mile had returned to watching cucumbers tumble down the various chutes and replacing the wooden crates when they were full.

"Hey, everybody," Agnes had said in a louder voice. This time everyone looked toward Agnes; they knew a story was coming. "You hear the one about the little old lady and the dentist?"

"Can't say that I have," George Roberts replied.

"Well, this little old lady, just a little thing no more than five feet or so tall, goes to the dentist to have a tooth filled. She don't like dentists—hard to find anybody who does, I guess. Anyway, she sits down in the chair and the dentist gets everthin' set.

"'You aren't gonna hurt me, are ya?' she asks.

"'This won't hurt a bit,' the dentist says, and he grabs the drill and leans over to start workin' on the tooth. Then he gasps and pulls back.

"'Lady,' he says, nearly whisperin'. 'You got hold of my privates.'

"'Yes, I know,' the sweet old lady says, smiling. 'We aren't going to hurt each other are we?'"

The dentist story had even gotten a smirk out of straight-laced Preacher.

At lunch, it was quiet for a time. Helen and the preacher were outside eating together. The rest of the crew sat around the sorter, eating their sack lunches, all except George Roberts. Andy figured he must have gone to the outhouse, which stood a hundred yards away from the factory under some trees and nearly out of sight.

Then they all heard a splash and someone shouting, "Help, help! I can't swim. I can't get out!" It was coming from the number-five pickle vat, which was in the far corner of the factory. They all ran to the vat and peered in. There was George Roberts, thrashing about with cucumbers and salt brine all around him. Helen and Preacher, hearing the ruckus, also rushed inside.

"I can't get out," George yelled. "I can't get out!"

Andy picked up a nearby broom and pushed the handle toward George. George grabbed on, and Andy pulled him close to the side of the vat. Preacher and Quarter Mile reached in, grabbed him under the arms, and dragged him onto the pickle factory floor.

"Tha' was a close one," George said, his words slurred. "About drownded, I did. About drownded in there."

"What were you doing, George?" Andy asked.

"Juss takin' a little nap. Crawled on top of the tank to take a little nap. Juss takin' a little nap," George said. "Musta fell through. That's it, musta fell through. Right in with those damn salty cukes."

"You're too heavy for those boards," Quarter Mile said. "Bad place to take a nap."

"Devil's got you in his clutches again," Preacher said, shaking his head.

"You been drinking, George?" Andy asked.

"Only a little swig, juss a little swig, 'nough to wet my whistle. Needed to wet my whistle."

"That isn't all you got wet, George," Quarter Mile offered.

"Must smell like . . . like a salted cuke," George said haltingly.

"You remember what I told you about drinking?" Andy said.

"Yeah, I 'member, 'member good. Real good. This mean I'm fired?"

"Yes, it does, George. You stop by the office, and Helen will write you a check. Sorry, George. You knew the rules."

"I did know the rules, Andy. Yes I did. I knew the rules. Needed to wet my whistle. Only wanted to wet my whistle."

George walked slowly toward the office, where Helen had already begun figuring out his wages. Pickle brine dripped from his clothing, leaving a little wet trail from the pickle vat to the factory office.

A moment later, George left the office and carefully climbed down the steps. He said nothing, and he didn't look back.

The crew watched him walk up the road that led away from the pickle factory. He had difficulty walking in a straight line.

Andy was already on the phone with Blackie Antonelli.

"How you feeling, Blackie?" Andy asked.

"Nose is pretty much healed. Still a little sore, but no swelling."

"You ready to go back to work?"

"You bet I am," Blackie replied.

"You gonna behave yourself?"

"Yeah," Blackie said in a rather noncommittal voice.

"Can you be here by four this afternoon?"

"I'll be there."

Blackie arrived a little before four. He said hello to Helen, shook Preacher's hand, shook Agnes's hand, and said "hi" to Quarter Mile Sweet.

"Lookin' better than last time I saw you," Blackie said, smiling.

"Same for you," Quarter Mile said. He was not smiling.

Before long the big red Ford truck from Stewart's farm arrived, slowly moving down the well-worn road to the factory. Carlos carefully backed the truck up to the platform, and Jesús Moreno and Alberto Torres quickly began tossing sacks of cucumbers.

"Hey, see you're back at work," Jesús said to Blackie.

"Yeah, I'm back."

"Have a good vacation?"

"Weren't no vacation."

"Heard it was," the young migrant said, taunting. It appeared these two were taking up where they had left off.

"Okay, boys," Andy said. "There's work to do."

Soon green cucumbers were tumbling over the sorter, but even before the first sack was completely dumped, Agnes said, "Stop the machine." Quarter Mile quickly flipped the switch.

"We got a problem," she said quietly to Andy. "See this, looks like that spot rot you told us about."

"That's it, all right," Andy said, shaking his head. "Everybody up to the sorter."

The entire crew, including Helen, slowly sorted the entire truckload of cucumbers, tossing out about a third of them. The factory crew helped the migrants re-sack the diseased cucumbers and load them back on the truck.

"Better ask Jake to come in tonight," Andy said to Carlos. "I'm afraid we've got a big problem."

"What's the problem?" Carlos asked.

"Diseased cucumbers. See these spots—they'll turn the whole cucumber to mush. Can't salt them. They'll all rot in the tanks. Spoil the other cucumbers, too," Andy said.

"Sí," Carlos said. "I'll tell Señor Jake to come along with the next load."

Andy hoped this would be the only time they'd see spot rot. Nevertheless, he got on the phone to J. W. Johnson.

"Think you better plan a trip over here after supper tonight," Andy said.

"What's going on? I haven't got time to run over to Link Lake tonight," Johnson said in his gravelly voice.

"Think we've got a spot-rot problem."

"Can't be."

"Sorted out about a third of Jake Stewart's first load today with spot rot. I said for Jake to come in tonight with the next load."

"Jake Stewart? He can't have a problem. You think there's a problem, you handle it," Johnson said gruffly.

"Think you better be here. In case we have to reject the whole load," Andy persisted.

"Think you're wrong, Meyer. Can't be nothin' the matter with Jake's cukes. He used our seed, our fertilizer, followed our orders to a T."

"I saw the spot-rot cukes, Mr. Johnson. They're bad."

"Oh, hell. I'll come. But it'll be a waste of time. I know Jake's got good cukes in those big fields."

The crew continued working through the afternoon, sorting the small batches of cucumbers that a few farmers brought in, not seeing any sign of spot rot. Around 6 p.m. Johnson roared up to the pickle factory in a cloud of dust and his usual bluster.

"You got some of them rotten cukes here?" he asked.

"Sent 'em all back to Jake's. Loaded them back on the truck. Wanted Jake to see what we'd done."

"Well, how in hell am I supposed to know if we got a problem if you ain't got any rotten cukes for me to look at?"

"I'm afraid you'll see all the spoiled cukes you want when Jake's next load gets here," Andy said.

A few minutes later, the big Ford truck returned, stacked high with sacks of Jake Stewart's cucumbers. Carlos eased the truck up to the loading dock, and then got out of the driver's side; Jake stepped down from the passenger side and immediately climbed the stairs to the factory floor.

Jake nodded to Andy and then said, "Hey there, Johnson. Glad you're here. What the hell is wrong? Mexicans brought back to the farm nearly as many cukes as they took." His voice was higher than normal, and he was leaning forward like he might fall on his face.

"I'm sure there's no problem, Jake. Let's get this truck unloaded," Johnson said to Carlos and the migrants riding on the back.

Andy flipped the switch and nodded to his entire crew to take their places at the sorter. Green cucumbers began bouncing toward their appropriate slots. The workers at the sorter tossed nearly every cucumber into the reject boxes. This load of cucumbers was even more infected than the previous one.

"Pull the switch," Andy said. The big machine shuddered to a stop.

Andy took a handful of diseased cucumbers over to J. W. Johnson and Jake Stewart. Jake had begun to perspire.

"See this," Andy said. He pointed to the small gray spots on each cucumber. Both men looked at the cucumbers but said nothing.

"Dump another three, four sacks and start the sorter," Johnson ordered. Once again, the crew tossed nearly all the cucumbers into the reject boxes. With the sorter clear, the crew waited for Johnson's decision. He brushed past Jake and Carlos and pulled the sorter switch himself. There was not a sound as everyone stood, watching him.

Then Jake, who was now perspiring heavily, spoke to J. W. Johnson. "They're just little spots. Can't be very serious. I did what you said. Planted them just like you suggested, cultivated and fertilized them just so, just like you wanted. Can't be anything wrong with these cucumbers."

"See these cukes? See them spots? They're rotten spots. In a few days the whole pickle will rot, and it'll spoil the good ones around it," Johnson said. His voice had taken on a new tone, more formal, more businesslike.

"But the spots are so little," Jake said plaintively.

"Doesn't matter. Spots start out small, get bigger. We're gonna have to turn back your whole load and shut you down."

"Shut me down?"

"Yup, that's what we gotta do, Mr. Stewart. As a representative of H. H. Harlow, I will not purchase these cucumbers."

"But I got a contract with you guys. Says you'll buy my cucumbers."

"Yes, you do, Mr. Stewart. But read that piece of paper. Says we won't buy any diseased cucumbers. And yours are diseased."

"The hell you say. You ain't buying any more of my cukes?" Jake was dumbfounded. "You gotta come out to the farm. See my fields. This is just a fluke."

"I don't think it's a fluke, Mr. Stewart. These cucumbers are infected, and we can't buy them," Johnson said.

"Just got to where I was makin' a little money and starting to pay off the seed and fertilizer loan to you guys. Just startin' to make a little money."

"Our company will not buy any rotten cucumbers," Johnson stated firmly.

"Well, son of a bitch," Jake said. "What a helluva note!"

"This isn't good for anybody," Andy said. "Sure hate to see this happen to you, Jake."

The rest of the factory crew was nearly as dumbfounded as Jake.

They stood around, looking at the floor and trying to keep their distance from the situation. Every one of them felt sorry for Jake. They knew how much money he had invested in his cucumber fields and how he had depended on the sale of cucumbers to ease himself out of debt. Preacher walked over to Jake and tried to put his hand on Jake's arm, but Jake brushed him off. Agnes said, "I'm sorry, Jake." But he didn't seem to hear her words.

"What'll I do with these guys?" Jake pointed toward the migrants, who were standing nearby, listening and wondering what was going on.

"H. H. Harlow will find another place for them," Johnson said. "Find some other cucumber fields that can use some late-season help."

"What's gonna happen to me?" Jake asked. He was red in the face, and his voice was higher than ever. His question hung unanswered in the humid night air.

To add to Jake's embarrassment, two days later the front-page story in the *Link Lake Gazette* carried the headline "Pickle King Dethroned." Jake wasn't happy about seeing his name in print, especially like this. He stormed into the newspaper office and slammed a copy of the paper down on the counter.

"I was expecting you'd be in," Dewey John said.

"Why in hell did you do this?" Jake asked, leaning forward as usual. His face was red.

"Jake, it's news. People deserve to know what happened."

"Just because that dumb county agent from Portage County found a few spots on my cucumbers and disqualified them?" Jake didn't mention that his cucumbers had been refused at the pickle factory on Monday.

"Yes, that makes news. Did you read the entire article, Jake?"

"Hell no. Headline made me so mad I didn't read any more."

"Well, read what I wrote about spot-rot disease and how it has devastated cucumber fields in Michigan. It's serious business," Dewey said.

Jake already knew how serious the problem was. He walked out of the newspaper office with his head down.

18

Love among the Pickle Vats

Word about what had happened at the factory spread like a blight. Whether they had a quarter acre or a couple acres of cucumbers, farmers wondered if spot rot would attack their pickle patch next. Ordinarily, the patches would produce for several more weeks. Now there was a better than average chance that many farmers would have to quit picking cucumbers early, plow their fields under, and hope they wouldn't be attacked again next year.

Only a few days after Jake Stewart's cucumbers were turned back, Andy had to refuse the Patterson family's five sacks. Slowly, more and more folks arrived with cucumbers showing the telltale spots. The country agent's words proved prophetic, and many farmers had to plow under what appeared to be perfectly good cucumber plants.

Of course the spot-rot problem affected the pickle factory as much as—or more than—it affected the farmers. When all the cucumber fields, big and little, were in full production, the factory crew worked well past midnight every night, sorting, weighing, and salting the day's intake. The H. H. Harlow Company always insisted that no fresh cucumbers sit overnight on the factory floor. According to Harlow policy all cucumbers and appropriate salt and water must be dumped into vats before the crew could go home. A factory manager would be fired if this rule were broken. The company prided itself on producing a quality product, and preserving fresh cucumbers as quickly as possible was one way to assure it.

With the spot-rot epidemic, the volume of cucumbers coming into the pickle factory slowed dramatically. Nonetheless, Agnes Swarsinski had never worked harder, inspecting each batch of cucumbers that tumbled over the sorter, looking for the telltale round, gray blotch, often no larger than the tip of a pencil eraser. When she spotted a diseased cucumber, she ordered the sorter stopped and the crew inspected each cucumber in the batch for infection. She could have merely said, "Spot-rot infection" and rejected the entire lot, but she saw the sad-faced farm boys and girls who had worked under a hot August sun and who were depending on the few dollars earned from their cucumbers to buy something special—a Red Ryder BB gun, a pair of ice skates, new shoes, or a new dress for school to replace the hand-me-downs from an older sister. She saw the kids' faces in her sleep, after she rejected their four or five sacks of spot-rot-infected cucumbers. She saw the disappointment in their eyes, sad eyes that knew their hard work was for nothing, eyes that asked why this one source of dependable money should be denied them because of something they did not do—because of some disease that had marched across the cucumber fields of Ames County.

When a grower with a half acre of cucumbers and a carload of kids arrived, the pickle factory workers inspected the cucumbers one at a time, tossing out the bad ones individually. Agnes and

Andy had an agreement, one they hadn't shared with J. W. Johnson. If more than half the cucumbers from one of these small acreage growers were disease free, the factory would buy the good cucumbers and the family would go home with something, even if it was only half of what they had expected. But if spot rot claimed more than half the lot, they had no choice but to reject the entire amount, and the farmer and his kids would return home with the same sacks of cucumbers they had delivered. A few kids burst into tears when Andy and Agnes rejected an entire load, but not many. Farm kids grew up with dashed dreams. The older ones had already learned to heed their elders' advice: "Never get your hopes up." They had learned to be surprised when things turned out better than they had planned, and they accepted disappointment with little comment, for it came often. Still, the bad news of rejected cucumbers was hard to swallow, for if anything came close to a sure thing it was growing and selling cucumbers to the Harlow pickle factory in Link Lake.

Of course when Jake Stewart's cucumbers came in with spot rot, Agnes and Andy rejected entire truckloads. Jake had insisted on sending cucumbers for a couple more days after J. W. Johnson had closed him down. Andy said it would be okay—that maybe in some of his several big fields the cucumbers would be free of spot rot. But they weren't. Jake's workers returned tons of fresh cucumbers to his farm and dumped them on the infected cucumber fields. Their angry eyes dug deep into Andy when he had to tell Carlos Rodríguez, who in turn told his workers, why their source of summer income had ceased, all due to a few spots of rot on every few cucumbers that bounced along the sorter.

"Are you sure?" Carlos had asked, quietly but firmly questioning Agnes's judgment.

"We're sure," Andy had said in an equally firm voice. "J. W. Johnson said absolutely no cucumbers with spot rot."

With the decision not to accept Jake's cucumbers, the volume delivered to the factory fell by a third. And with the rejection of several smaller growers, the cucumber volume fell to about one-fourth of what it had been but a week earlier. Andy heard that the Harlow Company had relocated the Rodríguez family and Jesús to a farm in a neighboring county that so far had avoided the spot-rot problem.

Andy began letting his crew go home early and come in late. On a drizzly foggy Wednesday, he let everyone go by four in the afternoon. He knew no one would pick cucumbers in the rain. He stayed on. He had office work to do, some reports that Helen had prepared for him to sign, and some repair work around the factory. Something was always breaking, it seemed. Andy had spotted a cracked board covering one of the pickle vats, and he decided to work on that first.

He remembered a small pile of boards stacked under the factory's main floor. Two doors allowed access to this shadowy area, where the rich smell of fermenting cucumbers was strong. Neither of the doors was locked, as there was nothing much to steal there, aside from a few boards and pickle-sorter parts.

When Andy entered the area, he noticed that the opposite door stood open. This was not especially unusual, as the town kids often snuck into this mysterious area to play tag, hide-and-seek, and other games. It was a wonderful place for hide-and-seek.

He heard giggling. As he had done once or twice before, he'd politely tell these kids that they shouldn't play here. They would leave—and of course they would return, because this was one of their favorite places.

Slowly Andy moved toward the giggling, hoping to surprise the kids and perhaps even scare them a little. He peered around a vat full of number-five cucumbers, and there on a blanket spread out between the vat holding gherkins and one storing number twos he spotted Helen Swanson and Preacher. They were both stark naked. She was giggling as he kissed her on the neck. He whispered something into her ear and she giggled even more.

Andy slowly backed away and quietly returned to the main floor of the factory. He had known that something more than counseling was going on between the preacher and Helen, but he didn't know it had come to this. After all, Preacher was married and had a houseful of kids—and he was a preacher. Word was that Preacher always spoke on the wages of sin and how sinners were destined to burn in hell. He had often preached on the most deadly sin of all, adultery. And here he was fooling around with Helen like he'd never uttered the words.

Andy wondered if he should say something to the both of them, let them know he had caught them in the act. Should he sit them down in the factory office and tell them he didn't approve of what they were doing, especially with Preacher being a married man with kids, and a man of the cloth besides?

He decided to keep quiet, at least for the time being. He thought that what they did on their own time was none of his business. As long as they came to work on time and did what they were supposed to while on the clock, he didn't care how they spent their off time. That's how he rationalized the situation, anyway.

But what Andy had seen stuck in his craw. What would Ethel Ketchum do when she found out, pious Ethel, who was quick to judge anybody in Link Lake whom she thought had stepped over the morality line, from those who cussed too much to those who regularly got drunk on Saturday night? And what about Preacher's kids? It was usually the kids who had the most to lose during these deals.

The following morning the entire factory crew reported for work promptly at nine, the new hour Andy had set. Helen arrived a few minutes early, and the preacher arrived on the stroke of nine.

Everyone was civil toward each other. Blackie Antonelli even said "good morning," something he seldom did. Perhaps the crew's behavior had something to do with getting a good night's sleep and the fact that within a few weeks Andy would roll shut the big doors, turn off the lights, snap the big brass padlock in place, and end another pickle season.

19

Missing Workers

Acouple of mornings after he caught Preacher and Helen among the pickle vats, Andy arrived at work to find Marshal Justin Quick's car parked by the loading ramp.

"Got a problem," Quick said as he climbed out of the squad car. Quick wore his big silver badge clipped to his belt, which he wore in an attempt to hold his ample middle in place as well as support a .38 revolver that hung low on his right side. He fumbled with the gun's worn wooden handle with one hand and pushed back his big white cowboy hat with the other.

"You know anything about Pastor Arthur Ketchum's whereabouts?"

"No, but I expect he'll be here in a few minutes," Andy answered.

"I'll just wait here, then," the marshal said. He put his fingers together and cracked his knuckles.

"What do you want with the preacher?" Andy asked.

"Just wanna know where he's at. His wife, Ethel, you know, the whiney one? Well, she called me this morning and said her husband hadn't gotten home last night. Got me out of bed, she did. She was all worked up, said it wasn't like him not to come home."

Soon the other workers began arriving. Blackie, Quarter Mile, and Agnes all arrived by nine, but no Preacher and no Helen Swanson, either.

"I'll wait a few minutes to see if he makes it," Marshal Quick said. He cracked his knuckles again.

By nine thirty neither of the two had arrived.

"Why don't you go over to Helen Swanson's house and check on her?" Andy said to the marshal.

Soon the marshal was back.

"House locked up tighter than a drum. Nobody home."

"You try to call Karl Swanson, her ex-husband?" Andy asked.

"Nah, no use. Last I heard he moved to Chicago," Quick answered.

"Better come into the office," Andy said, motioning for the marshal to come up the steps. Andy realized he had better not keep secret what he knew about Helen and Preacher. He closed the office door. Marshal Quick pulled a little notebook from his shirt pocket and flipped it open. "I'm ready for your statement," he said, very officially. "Haven't had a missing person case in a long while."

"Helen was having lots of problems since her divorce," Andy began.

"Yup," the marshal said. He took off his big hat and tossed it into a corner.

"Preacher agreed to give her some counseling," Andy said.

"Counseling, huh?" A slow smile spread over the marshal's face.

"Besides that, at the beginning of the season the preacher tried to get the crew to pray before lunch. You can imagine how that went over," Andy continued. "Anyway, the preacher and Helen began eating their lunches together, and before you could say amen and hallelujah, Helen joined his Church of the Holy Redeemed."

"One thing led to another, huh?"

"Those are the facts. But off the record, I don't want you spreading the next part around," Andy said, though he knew full well the marshal probably would.

"Oh, no, never do that." The marshal put down his pad and leaned in closer.

"Yesterday I saw the two of them buck-naked downstairs between the pickle vats, closer together than they ought to be."

"The preacher! That's a tough one to swallow," Quick said.

"Well, it's the truth."

The marshal leaned back in his chair. "Same old story. Heard it a hundred times. Little different with a preacher involved."

"Remember, you said you'd keep this part to yourself," Andy reminded Quick.

"Oh, yeah, wouldn't want to spread that kind of information around. 'Fore you know it, that place downstairs around the pickle tanks will get a reputation," the marshal laughed.

"You know what I mean, Marshal. Think of the preacher's kids."

"Yeah, the preacher's kids."

"So it looks like they up and ran off together," Andy said.

"Looks that way. Sure looks that way."

"So what're you gonna do?"

"Nothin'. Nothin' I can do. No crime committed. Nobody kidnapped. Nobody robbed—unless you might say Helen was robbed, but it sounds like she was givin' it away."

"So you aren't doing anything?"

"Nope. Not until I hear some crime's been committed. People runnin' off together ain't no crime. Not here in Link Lake anyway," the marshal said.

"Sure as anything Ethel'll want some answer from me. What do I tell her?" Andy asked.

"Say whatever you want. Facts seem clear. They had a thing for each other and they ran away. That's what I'll tell her, anyway." The marshal leaned over and picked up his hat, stood up, hitched up his belt, cracked his knuckles, and was on his way out. "I'll let you know if I hear anything."

By now the first load of cucumbers had arrived, six sacks that the farmer hoisted up on the loading dock from the back of his old car, from which he had removed the back seat.

"Got a problem here?" the farmer asked when he saw the marshal leaving in his squad car.

"Nah, just a little misunderstanding," Andy said. He knew that the news of the preacher running off with the bookkeeper would fly around Link Lake faster than a tornado in June. And he knew the stories would start the minute Marshal Quick returned to his office. Quick had a reputation for being the best news source in the area. Especially when it came to what made the juiciest gossip—who was arrested for drunkenness, who was beating his wife, which kids in town were the most troublesome, and, of course, the most outstanding news of all: which married men were messing around with other women. He even knew who wasn't paying their bills, who had passed a bad check or two, or who had trouble paying their taxes. But that kind of news was on the boring order, compared to men jumping over the traces with other women.

After the farmer left, Andy quietly told the pickle factory crew what he believed had happened. He spared them the details of what he had seen between the pickle vats.

"Saw them going at it a couple weeks ago," Agnes said. "I'm not surprised they ran off together."

Andy said he hoped the two of them would come back, especially Helen, because now he had to do all the bookwork himself, write the checks, figure the salt, and keep all the records. It would be impossible to hire a competent person this late in the season.

That afternoon a newer blue Buick car pulled up to the pickle factory. Four big women wearing flowered dresses and hats piled out and walked single file from the car to the factory steps. Andy saw them coming. They looked familiar—they were the same women he'd seen on the parade float trying to sing hymns. They were like four big ducks waddling in a row, one right after the other. On a mission, looking for some answers.

One after the other, they marched up the steps and across the factory floor to where the crew was working.

"I'm looking for Andy Meyer," the lead duck said. It was obvious that her feathers were ruffled.

"I'm Andy."

"I am Prudence Wordsworthy of the Church of the Holy Redeemed. We need to have a talk." She did not extend a hand.

"Sure, go ahead."

"Can we talk privately?" Prudence asked. When she spoke she twitched so that the big colorful flowers on her hat vibrated.

"How about in the office?"

Andy led the way, and the four women, still in single file, paraded behind him. It reminded him a little of his days in the army, when everybody walked in a straight line, in step.

Andy shut the door. He offered the two chairs in the office, but the foursome refused to sit, so Andy took the chair by the desk. The office was fairly bursting with heavily perfumed, big women.

"What can I do for you?" Andy asked.

"As I said, we are from the Church of the Holy Redeemed."

It was already getting warm in the little office, and the heavy smell of perfume was giving Andy a headache.

"I believe you know our beloved preacher, Arthur Ketchum?"

"Yes, I know him well. He's worked here all summer."

"Well, that certainly has been a mistake. He never should have sought outside employment. He should have said he couldn't make ends meet. The ladies of the church would have helped him out and made sure he got a few more potatoes, a half a hog, or an extra sack of rutabagas. We could have helped him out. He didn't need to work here."

"He turned out to be a good worker."

"That Helen Swanson works here too, doesn't she?" the head duck asked.

"Yes, she does," Andy said.

"She's been a member of our church for only a short time. What do you know of her background? Why did she get divorced? What does she do here? Why would a woman work in a place like this anyway?" the head duck snarled.

"She is our bookkeeper, and a darn good one, too," Andy said, raising his voice a little.

"You watch your language, young man. There will be no coarse language in our presence."

"Sorry," Andy said, not sure what he had said that was considered coarse.

"We may have misjudged that Helen," the short duck hissed.

"That woman, that harlot," the lead duck sputtered. "She's the one responsible for all this."

"That's what happens when an upstanding church like ours accepts a divorced woman into its midst," the second duck hissed. She pulled a dainty handkerchief from her sleeve and dabbed her forehead.

"That Helen, she's the one responsible for all this," said the third duck, who had previously not spoken. She barely opened her mouth when she talked, so the words came out a bit garbled.

"Responsible for what?" Andy asked.

"You know full well. You know what was going on between that seducer and our spiritual leader. You knew what was going on," the lead duck chimed in as she wagged her long crooked finger in Andy's face. "Don't you know how to control your help? Can't you keep your employees in order and show them how to walk down a Christian path?"

"Didn't think it was any of my business what path they chose."

"Well, it should have been your business. If you'd been doing your job, leading your people in the way of the Lord, this wouldn't have happened," the lead duck said in a too-loud voice.

"It's sad, so sad what this Helen did to our beloved preacher," the short duck said. She was shaking her head back and forth vigorously. Andy wondered if her big hat would remain in place.

"So sad," the second duck said.

"So sad," the third duck mumbled.

Just then came a loud knock on the office door and Blackie Antonelli stuck in his head. "Andy, where in hell are the extra pickle crates?"

153

"Humph," the lead duck said as she bristled and ruffled her feathers. "You will not speak such words in the presence of Christian women," she huffed.

"Oh, sorry," Blackie said to the woman, whose face was red. He turned again to Andy. "Where in hell are the extra crates?"

"Back of the salt bin," Andy answered.

"Is he . . . is he an example of the kind of help you have here?" Prudence Wordsworthy was trying to catch her breath.

"Blackie's a good worker. Swears a little too much, but he works hard."

"How do you put up with having such a longhaired heathen in your midst? Oh, poor pastor. No wonder he strayed. No wonder he allowed the wiles of a dangerous woman to lead him off the path. Working around heathens everyday. Oh, the poor man. The poor man, whatever has become of him? Whatever has become of him?" the lead duck asked.

"Oh, the poor man," the third duck mumbled.

"Oh, the poor man," the second duck added.

"Oh, the poor man," the little duck concluded.

To Andy it sounded like a barnyard chorus, with each woman repeating what the previous one had just said.

"You know, it often takes two people for these things to happen," Andy broke in.

"Oh, how could you even suggest that our beloved pastor had anything to do with this, a man of the cloth? An esteemed follower of the word?" The lead duck asked.

"Preacher must have gotten another word from Helen," Andy said. He knew it was a mistake to say it the moment the words left his mouth.

The lead duck's nose flew in the air. "You . . . you, young man, are without respect. We are talking about a man of God, not some everyday worker at this despised place of employment."

"He was just another worker when he was here, a pretty good one, too. Did his work well." Andy was biting his tongue not to tell off these pious old busybodies.

"Oh, how could he? How could he work around these Godless people?" A chorus of "how could he's" bounced off the walls of the little office.

"This bookkeeper . . . this seducer has obviously stolen our pastor from us, taken him away to some heathen place. Ah, but he is a strong man; he will resist the temptations of a harlot. We all know he will."

Andy resisted the temptation to smile. He considered sharing what he had seen between the pickle vats, but he thought better of it. In his mind he saw the four of them fainting dead away at the very idea. Then he would be faced with hauling four heavily perfumed, pious women out of the pickle factory. Nobody would want such a task.

"What are you doing about all this?" the head duck asked loudly. She was beginning to perspire heavily, dabbing at her wet brow with a little white handkerchief.

"Don't think there is anything I can do. Sounds like they ran off together."

"For heaven's sake, don't you have anybody out looking for them?"

"Where would we look?"

"You must know these places, you must know."

"Well, *I don't* know these places," Andy said. He was becoming perturbed. "I've got to get back to work," he said as he stood and opened the door.

"Well, I do declare," the lead duck said as she pranced out the door. "I do declare." The other three fell in line behind her, and they marched across the floor down the stairway, the lead one nearly tripping on the bottom step. They stomped in single file to the Buick, quickly crawled in, and slammed the doors in unison. The car's rear wheels threw gravel against the side of the pickle factory wall as it roared up the driveway.

20

Breaking News

Marshal Quick kept no secrets. When he had news, he shared it. It's hard to say whether Quick saw it as a civic duty to keep people informed or was a gossip who couldn't keep a story to himself. Of course, he was also looking for some publicity, because he was up for reelection.

The marshal detailed the disappearance of the preacher and the bookkeeper to Dewey John at the *Link Lake Gazette* office right after he talked with Andy. He said he was mounting an investigation to make sure there had been no wrongdoing and that no harm had come to either Preacher or Helen.

"It's the biggest story of the year," the marshal said. "Maybe the biggest story in five years."

Dewey listened carefully but didn't comment.

The marshal took time explaining what Andy Meyer had said about what happened between the pickle vats in the factory cellar. As he listened, he wondered if the good marshal expected him to write about the fornication right down to its naked details. Dewey tried to keep from smiling as the marshal went on and on, as only he was capable of doing.

"You'll wanna feature this on the front page of the paper," the marshal said. "And I'm ready to pose for a photo if you want one."

"Not right now," Dewey said, trying not to laugh.

"Okay, then," the marshal said. "Just let me know when you want a photo—or another interview." He gathered up his hat, cracked his knuckles, and left.

Looking out the window, Dewey noticed that Marshal Quick stopped at the Link Lake Tap on his way down Main Street. More news was digested, discussed, cussed, and created there than almost any other place in town—his challenge was to report this runaway incident accurately without fueling the gossip machine, which had already shifted into high gear.

The editor decided to drive over to the pickle factory and talk with Andy, to get his version of the story. When he did, he found that what the marshal had said mostly jibed with Andy's description, except for the part about the investigation. The marshal had told Andy he wasn't going to do anything about the disappearance, because two people could run off together and not break any laws.

Now Dewey was faced with how to report all this in the paper. Villages like Link Lake have several news sources, the newspaper being only one of them, and often the least significant. The news that traveled by word of mouth, in the taverns, at the feed mill, at the cheese factory, in the mercantile—this mattered most to the residents of the Link Lake community. The rumor mill was where all the juicy stuff was passed along, all the details, whether accurate or manufactured, all the gore, the indiscretion, all of it.

In the minds of the locals, the newspaper seldom reported anything new. Rather, they saw it as a confirmation. "See, I told you. Here it is in the paper. Right here in the paper." Once something was printed there, it was viewed as the absolute truth, never to be questioned.

Dewey decided to report the preacher and Helen's disappearance on page two. He didn't detail the couple's antics, the details everyone was drooling to read. The older women would sniff at the awfulness of it all, and a few would secretly wonder if they could have an adventure like this. There was a certain romance to falling in love among pickle vats, the air heavy with the smell of fermenting cucumbers. Of course, some of the men had openly discussed what it would be like to run off with a pretty blond divorcée.

Dewey had bigger news to report on page one. Unfortunately, because of the pickle factory affair holding everyone's attention, no one was talking about the real pickle problem. The spot-rot epidemic had decimated the cucumber crop in the area. It continued to close down the little patches. This would mean a smaller pile of Christmas presents under the trees this winter, fewer kids with new clothes for school, and many promises of new bicycles being put off for yet another year.

Front-page news also included the upcoming election in the Rose Hill School District. People would be voting on consolidation in a special election scheduled for Tuesday, September 6, at the Rose Hill Town Hall.

Often the paper took a stand on the *Gazette*'s editorial page arguing for how people should vote. This time it didn't. For his front-page story, Dewey John tried to collect as much information as he could. It was a tough assignment because he had never seen an issue divide a community so completely. He wrote about the pluses for consolidation—an improved science program (a laboratory), the opportunity for children to play in a band, a stronger math program, more expansive social study opportunities, and teachers who could concentrate on one or two grades rather than all eight.

On the other side of the issue he noted that when country-school pupils entered high school they almost always did as well as, and often better than, the town kids. The country-school kids learned how to study by themselves. And they could progress according to their own abilities. If they were in fourth grade and good at reading, they might sit with the fifth or even sixth grade reading groups. Same with arithmetic, writing, and social studies. Country-school kids also helped younger students having difficulties in all sorts of subjects, both in the classroom and outside the school. For instance, it was not unusual for an eighth grade student to show a first grader how to hold a bat and hit a softball.

Dewey wrote about the advantages of walking to and from school and how much cheaper it was for children to walk than ride a bus. And he noted the importance of country schools to their communities, how a country school gave a rural community an identity, including a name, along with a center for social activities.

After the story appeared on August 31, the paper received a pile of letters to the editor. Many were filled with too much profanity to print. Some letter writers argued the county school must remain open at all costs: "The Rose Hill school was good enough for my grandpa, good enough for my pa, good enough for me, and good enough for my kids. Why change?"

Others took up the tax question, saying that even though the consolidated school promised lower taxes, the evidence they had heard from neighboring communities whose schools had closed was that taxes had shot up. Still others wrote about the great changes occurring in the state and how rural children needed a better education to be prepared for the future.

Even more vocal were Jake Stewart, who was clearly for consolidation, and Isaac Meyer, who was clearly against it. Both had traveled around the school district over the past few weeks, stopping at other farms and making their positions known. Emotions ruled, and facts played a minor role. Jake Stewart, as school board president, asked Marshal Quick if he would spend election day at the town hall. "Just park yourself out front and make sure people behave themselves," Jake told the marshal.

Of course the marshal was glad to oblige—it was one more way for the public to see him. On election day, the marshal wore a freshly pressed uniform and a specially cleaned white hat, and he had even shined his badge, which he wore on his shirt this day. His .38 revolver was clearly visible. As voters entered the town hall, the marshal said "howdy" and shook their hands. This behavior was probably not what Jake had in mind when he asked the marshal to spend the day at the town hall; it looked ever so much like politicking (which it was) than policing (which seemed hardly necessary).

Cars lined both sides of the road trailing past the Rose Hill Town Hall when Dewey John stopped by that Tuesday afternoon. People with glum faces filed out of the building, having voted but still not knowing their neighbors' positions.

At eight o' clock that night, with the votes counted, the school board clerk tacked the results on the town hall door:

For consolidation and closing of Rose Hill School—60

Against consolidation and closing of Rose Hill School—59

The seventy-five-year-old school would complete one more school year, and then the school buses would rumble down the back roads of the former Rose Hill District and the little school would close its doors for good. For Dewey John, the vote was one sign of how rural communities were changing.

The news was huge for the people living in the district. Not only would they have to adjust to their school closing, but, more importantly, they would have to mend the split in their community. Such healing would be difficult, perhaps impossible.

21

Auction

Allan Clayton's fatal heart attack in mid-August had come as a surprise to everyone. Just two days before he died, he had delivered a pickup load of cucumbers to the pickle factory, and he and Andy had talked about what it was like ten years ago, when World War II had ended and farmers were just getting back on their feet. He had seemed perfectly healthy, tall, thin, and trim. He had told Andy he was planning to increase the size of his cucumber patch to maybe an acre next year, as long as the price of cukes stayed reasonably good.

Andy said he had no idea about next year's cucumber prices, but was pleased the prices had stayed up during the current season. "Price depends on lots of things—how pickles are selling, how many tons of pickles Harlow has in stock, how the cucumber crop is in other states."

The two neighbors talked for more than a half hour as Clayton's cucumbers were sorted and weighed, and the check was made out.

"You planning to stay on the home farm, Andy?" Allan had asked.

"Yup, I plan to do that."

"You're different from my kids. They got to be city people. Seem to like it in the city. Like the bright lights, I guess," Allan said, laughing.

"Sounds like they're doing well, making lots of money."

"That they are," Allan said. "But there's more to life than making money. Something about living on the land that's in my blood."

"Mine, too," Andy said. "I could never leave the farm, funny as it may sound."

"There's not many young people like you anymore," Allan said, folding his cucumber check and putting it in the top pocket of his bib overalls. "Don't know what's going to happen to this country. Young people moving off the land. People like Jake Stewart buying up hundreds of acres."

Now the bill for the Clayton auction had been thumbtacked to the pickle-factory bulletin board for a week. Andy studied it nearly every morning when he came to work. He couldn't believe that his friend had died, just like that. With no warning. Andy had gone to school with the Clayton kids: Henry, now an attorney in Milwaukee; and Cindy, an accountant in Madison. The two kids couldn't wait to graduate from high school so they could leave the farm; it was obvious that they wouldn't be coming back to take over the home place. Iris, Allan's wife of forty years, had no choice but to sell. She planned to move to Madison and live with her daughter.

1955 Season
Auction
Mrs. Allan Clayton, Link Lake, Wisconsin

Auction

Reason for sale: Death of Mr. Clayton.
Country Trunk A west four miles from Link Lake,
then north a mile to the farm.
Saturday, September 10
Sale to start at 11:30 a.m. Lunch on the grounds.
Farm will be sold at 3:00 p.m.
Terms: Cash

The sale bill went on to list machinery: Farmall H tractor, International quack digger, 3-section roll-up drag, Oliver 2–14″ plow w. Raydex points, John Deere low-wheeled 8 ft. grain drill with fertilizer and grass seed attachment. Two-section springtooth harrow. John Deere semi-mounted mower, 7 ft. cut. 4-wheel wagon and good hayrack. Case 8 ft. grain binder. Horse potato digger. New Idea manure spreader, John Deere 8 ft. tandem disc. Two-row horse corn planter. Dump rake. Hay loader and smaller items too numerous to mention.

In addition to the machinery, the auction bill listed fifteen mixed-breed milk cows, a team of draft horses, and a 1948 Chevrolet pickup truck, plus several miscellaneous items: a thousand pound scale, stock tank, scalding kettle, 120 feet of $1\frac{1}{4}$ inch hayfork rope, eight milk cans, three bundles of new steel fence posts, chicken brooder, three cords of oak chunk wood, and a milk cart.

The day of the auction was clear, cool, and bright. The hot spell that had settled over Link Lake for the past week or so had moved on east and cooler, drier weather had moved in.

By 10:30 that Saturday morning, cars were parked on both sides of the road so that latecomers had to walk nearly a quarter mile to the farmstead. All the machinery was lined up in neat rows in a field near the road. The cows, each with a numbered sticker on her back end, were in the barn — usually they would be

165

out on pasture this time of the year. Allan Clayton's prized team of Percherons, which he had often driven in parades, stood in their stalls. They, too, would normally have been out to pasture or doing some task such as pulling the dump rake or the manure spreader. Since Allan had gotten a tractor a few years ago, most of the heavy work such as plowing, cutting hay and grain, and disking was left to the tractor.

A hay wagon had been pulled in front of the open machinery shed door and was piled high with pitchforks, nuts, bolts, hammers, wrenches, old barn lanterns, hay-fork pulleys, a length of hay-fork rope, curry combs for the horses, a partly used can of fly spray, an empty five-gallon gas can, two cans of unopened grease, a grease gun, three garden hoes, a couple axes, and a two-man crosscut saw, plus several coffee cans filled with assorted nails, bolts, nuts, and staples for repairing wire fences.

Promptly at 11:30 the auctioneer, Colonel Stanford S. Strong, climbed onto the wagon. He wore a big white hat, cowboy boots, and a belt with a huge silver buckle that struggled against his ample stomach.

"It's about time we got started," he said in a hoarse voice. "Got lots of items to sell today. Here are the rules. All sales are cash on the spot; you settle up with the clerk over there." He pointed to a man seated at a card table under a tree. "You buy it, and it's yours."

Henry Clayton was helping out and looking quite uncomfortable wearing bib overalls. He handed the auctioneer a long-handled hoe that had obviously spent many hours in a cucumber patch, as the handle was worn smooth and the blade was about half the size it would have been when it was new.

"What am I offered for this good hoe?" Strong began. "Everybody can use a good hoe. Do I hear two dollars, two dollars, two dollars, anybody two dollars for this good hoe? Two dollars, two dollars, two dollars." Pause. "Anybody a dollar?"

"Dollar," somebody near the front said as he held up his hand.

"Got a dollar, now make it two, two dollar, two dollar, anybody make it two? Two, two, two. I'm gonna sell it for a dollar. Last chance. Anybody two? Sold, to this man up front who knows a bargain when he sees one."

So the sale went on, item by item, bid by bid, a quarter here, a dollar there—the tools of farming offered for sale: hammers and saws, barbed wire and crowbars, axes and splitting wedges, kerosene barn lanterns and cowbells. A wagonload of memories, each item with a story to tell, now sold as just another commodity, another piece of equipment that a new owner would find useful.

A covey of antique buyers watched with interest and bid often, buying farm tools that would never find a home on a workbench again but would sit on a table in an antique store, crowded together with Depression glass, World War I insignia, old dolls, and toys.

With the wagonload of equipment sold, the auctioneer crawled down from his perch and announced, "We'll sell the cattle next." He walked off toward the barnyard where people had already gathered along the once-white fence.

A young Holstein heifer, with a paper number, twenty-two, pasted on her rump, stood a few feet from the fence with her head down, eyeing the crowd and not knowing whether to run or hold her ground.

"Got this nice heifer, here. She's a good one. Anybody tryin' to improve their herd can't go wrong with this one." He launched into his singsong chant, "And what am I offered for this good heifer? Who'll give me a hunnert for her, do I hear a hunnert, anybody got a hundred dollar bill for this fine little Holstein?"

A man in the back held up his hand.

"And who'll make it two, two, two, two, who'll make it two hundred dollars for this little Holstein heifer? Make somebody a good milker. Look at that conformation, look at them legs. She's got good legs. Gonna hold up for a long time, be in somebody's barn for a good long time. Got one who'll make it two?"

"Hunnert and a half," a fellow in the front row said.

"And now two?" The auctioneer looked at the fellow who'd made the first bid. The fellow nodded yes.

"And now two-fifty?" This time the auctioneer peered down at the fellow in the front row, who shook his head no.

"I got two, who'll make it two-fifty, two-fifty, two-fifty?"

Neither the auctioneer nor the crowd saw the little gray-haired woman standing near the farmhouse porch, watching the sale from a distance, tears streaming down her face. Iris Clayton stood alone, watching her life on the farm being sold piece by piece, animal by animal. Memories flooded over her, of milking the cows that now were numbered to be sold—cows that she knew by name, Susan and Florence, Sally and Lilly, Amanda and Polly. She knew each one, knew her personality, how she wanted to be milked, what she liked to eat, how much milk she gave. Information that no one else cared about, private information that she held and cherished. *How do you sell a memory?* she wondered. The tears continued down her face.

"Iris, you alright?" a neighbor woman asked.

"Got some dust in my eyes," Iris answered. It was difficult for her to share her grief, to let others know she couldn't handle something as simple as an auction.

Later in the afternoon, after the cows had been auctioned and the horses and the big machinery were gone and the plows and disc, the old grain binder, the Farmall H tractor with its cultivator attached all sold, the auctioneer announced to the crowd that remained. "We're gonna sell the farm now. What we got here is one hundred sixty acres of land. About hunnert and forty is tillable; the rest is woods. And the buildings, of course, go with it. Got this fine house and barn, and all these outbuildings—some of these could use some repair. Wouldn't want to lie to you about that. Corncrib needs a new roof, so does the granary. Rest are in fair shape, I'd say.

"Anyway, who'll give me an offer? Who'll give me seven thousand for this fine farm? The Claytons took good care of it. Raised their kids, even made enough to send them off to college. This is a good farm. And, who'll start with seven thousand? Do I hear seven thousand?"

"Six thousand," a man no one recognized said. He stood in the front row and wore bib overalls, a plaid shirt, and a John Deere cap.

"Got six thousand, who'll make it seven? Got six, who'll make it seven. Seven, seven, seven."

A hand went up in the back of the small crowd of people gathered around the auctioneer.

"Seven thousand," the man said. It was another stranger. He was wearing a hat, the kind you wore to church on Sunday, and a leather vest.

"I got seven thousand, who'll make it eight?" The auctioneer looked at the man in the front row.

"Eight," the man said.

"Got eight, who'll make it nine. Do I hear nine?"

"Nine," the man with the fancy hat and leather vest said.

"Got nine, anybody for ten? Ten, ten?" Once again the auctioneer looked at the man in the front row. The auctioneer knew that this farm was not worth a penny over seven thousand dollars. The man shook his head, no.

Later, the community learned that the mysterious buyer lived in Milwaukee and he'd purchased the land for hunting. He had no interest in farming at all. Later that fall, he invited the Link Lake Fire Department to come out and burn the buildings, as a practice event—property taxes on the land would of course be lower with the buildings gone. Many memories went up in smoke the day the Claytons' farmstead buildings burned.

22

Jake Stewart

The week of the Clayton auction, the "letters to the editor" section of the *Link Lake Gazette* was nearly bursting with commentary about recent events.

A young girl, upset about the spot-rot problem, wrote:

Dear Editor:

My two brothers and two sisters and I have an acre pickle patch that our pa gave us. He said we could keep half the money we earned, as long as we did all the hoeing and weeding. We all worked hard, even my youngest sister who is only three years old came out to the patch to help. Our cucumbers grew real good, and they produced lots of cukes, too. Then the spot rot came and the pickle factory people wouldn't buy our cucumbers anymore. What are we supposed to do? Now we kids have no money. Pa and Ma needed the money too. It's just not fair."

Sincerely,
Amy Wilson, age 12

Everyone's heart went out to that little girl and her family. But she was only one of many kids in the Link Lake community who were feeling the sting of a shortened cucumber season.

Dewey John expected several letters from the people in the Rose Hill School District after the election. But there wasn't a peep out of those folks; they apparently had chosen to fight their battles among themselves and keep their disagreements out of the newspaper.

That wasn't the case with the "Preacher affair," as people referred to it. One letter writer accused the paper of whitewashing the whole thing. This person started off with "Dear editor: Your paper has sold out to H. H. Harlow." How in the world this person came to that conclusion escaped Dewey John. She slammed the paper for its "continuing big business bias."

Another writer went after young Andy Meyer: "The manager of the pickle factory is not able to control his workers. Andy Meyer has allowed the pickle factory to become a love nest. He has lost control of his small staff of workers and should be fired. Anyone who allows such immorality to take place has no right to manage anything. H. H. Harlow should replace him, and quickly, before we hear of some other scandal at the pickle factory."

Still another critic, a member of the Church of the Holy Redeemed, mailed the paper a four-page tirade that began:

To whom it may concern:

> That harlot bookkeeper at the Harlow pickle factory seduced a popular area preacher and noted spiritual leader right under the less-than-watchful eyes of the factory manager. Mr. Andy Meyer has failed his Christian duty to maintain a Christian purpose and a God-fearing atmosphere at this historic Link Lake establishment. The pickle factory manager has tarnished the reputation of our fine village, and has put our entire congregation in a state of mourning at the loss of their revered pastor.

Dozens of letters like these piled up on Dewey John's desk. He'd never seen anything like it. Tangle a preacher in a sex affair, and pens and paper come out and the comments fly. Few people seemed concerned about what had happened to the couple or where they had run off to. Neither of their cars was missing, the depot agent said neither of them had bought rail tickets, and the Greyhound office in Plainfield had no record of them purchasing bus tickets. Marshal Quick concluded that a long-distance trucker had picked them up and took them who knew where. A story began circulating that around the time of Preacher's and Helen's disappearance, a white eighteen-wheeler that had delivered a load of lumber to the Link Lake Lumber Company was seen leaving town with more than one person in the cab.

Helen's neighbor, Abigail Martin, told another version of what happened. "I saw a big black car pull up in front of Helen's house in the dead of night. I think it had Illinois license plates—and it looked like a mobster's car," Abigail said. When Marshal Quick asked her why she thought it was a mobster's car, she said, "Well, the car was big, it was black, and it was night." She didn't recall whether anyone had gotten in or out of the vehicle. "But it surely looked suspicious, very suspicious."

Karl Swanson, Helen's ex-husband? The marshal thought. He tucked the idea in the back of his mind for further consideration.

A couple weeks after J. W. Johnson refused to buy Jake's cucumbers, Jake stopped at the Link Lake National Bank and asked to see his old friend, Amos Caldwell, whom he had known since they were kids.

"Amos," Jake said in his high-pitched voice. "I'm in a bit of a pickle, what with Harlow refusing to buy any more of my cucumbers."

"Heard about that, Jake. Damned shame, that spot rot coming in and wiping out your crop. Terrible thing."

"Had thirty acres you know, and they was doin' purty good—got to the point where I had nearly paid off Harlow's loans for fertilizer, seed, and haulin' the migrants up here from Texas. Just about ready to make a little money, I was. Then bam, I'm out of the cucumber business." Jake clapped his hands together for emphasis.

"It's a shame, Jake. Dirty shame. How can I help you today?"

"Looks like I'm gonna need a little extension on my mortgage payment comin' due next month. Was countin' on the pickle money, and now there ain't no more pickle money."

Amos Caldwell paged through a thick file he had in front him on his big, oak desk. Papers piled high on both sides of the desk left but a small clear area in the center. Behind the desk, a window provided a view of the waters of Link Lake, blue and inviting.

"We've got a lot of money in your operation," Amos said, looking over glasses that hung on the end of his long nose. His bald head shined with perspiration.

"I know that," Jake said quietly, almost in a whisper. "I know that. Always made my mortgage payments."

"Not quite true, Jake. Remember two years ago, when we had that dry spell and your corn crop didn't amount to much? You were six months late."

"Yeah, that's right. Kind of forgot about that."

Amos Caldwell rubbed his hand across his head and then closed the folder in front of him.

"I'm afraid we can't give you an extension, Jake. Sorry to say that. But we are way over our loan limit with you—we were counting on your cucumber crop, too."

"You mean that's it—you won't give me an extension after all we've been through together? We've known each other a long time—you can't just cut me off."

"Can't help it, Jake. We've got rules to follow, and I've already stretched them way too far in your case."

"So what am I supposed to do? "What can I do?" Jake asked, quietly. He was rubbing his hands together.

"I frankly don't know," Amos said. "But I've got to tell you that unless the bank gets a mortgage payment this fall, we'll have to start foreclosure proceedings on you."

"Foreclose on me?"

"Afraid so. Wouldn't be my choice. I'd argue against it. But rules are rules."

"Some kind of friend you are," Jake said, standing up quickly. "Some kind of friend."

"I'm sorry, Jake. Really sorry."

"I'll bet you are. You damned money people are all the same. Lookin' out for your own skins first, to hell with what happens to us poor farmers." Jake spun around, left the office, and drove out of town.

Upon his arrival at home, he noticed a big green Cadillac parked in the yard, under the elm tree that shaded his back porch. On the doors of the car were the words "H. H. Harlow Pickle Company." The car must have just arrived, as dust still hung in a cloud over the gravel road.

As Jake approached, a tall young man wearing a white shirt and a green tie stepped out of the car.

"You Jake Stewart?" the man said, smiling. He had a friendly way about him. His shiny brown shoes and white shirt contrasted with Jake's denim overalls and chambray work shirt.

"Yup, that's me," Jake said.

"Name is Henry Harlow," the man said. "I'm from the H. H. Harlow Pickle Company." He extended his hand, as did Jake.

"Nice day," Harlow said.

"Guess so," Jake answered. "Hadn't really noticed. Got other things on my mind."

"I know about your cucumber fields," Harlow said. "Shame. Just a shame what happened to you."

"Yeah, just when I was startin' to make some money and pay off my debt to you guys."

"I'm here to talk about next year," Harlow said. "There is always another year."

"Might not be another year for me," Jake blurted out. "Bank's plannin' on foreclosin' on me. Had counted on the cucumber money to make the mortgage payment."

"Didn't know about that," the young Harlow said. "Tell you what: I think I may have an answer for you."

"I'm a listenin'," Jake said.

"You're planning on growing cucumbers with us again next year, aren't you?" Harlow asked. He had an intense look in his eyes.

"Haven't decided yet."

"Oh, you can't let one year get you down!" the young man said enthusiastically.

"I can if it works out like this one did."

"Here's what we'll do." Harlow paused for a moment.

"Yeah?" said Jake.

"If you plant fifty acres of cucumbers next year . . ."

"Fifty acres? I'm losin' my shirt with thirty."

"This year was a fluke. We've got new seeds that are resistant to spot rot—developed right down there at the College of Agriculture in Madison. You won't have that problem again. Guaranteed."

"Guaranteed, huh? What do I have to do?"

"Well, you sign a contract with us for fifty acres. We'll provide you with all the seed, all the fertilizer, and arrange for the migrants—at our reasonable prices, of course. And we'll roll over the money you owe us until next year—you'll pay a little interest."

"Yeah, well all that does is put me further behind and owing you more money. And where am I gonna get the money to make my mortgage payments this fall?"

"And we'll also lend you whatever you need to make your mortgage payments—at reasonable interest rates. And you don't have to pay us a thing until your crop comes in. You won't owe us a cent until next fall, a year from now."

"I'll . . . I'll have to think that over. Have to think that over," Jake said. "Does sound like a good deal, though."

"Good deal. You bet it is. You'll be the biggest cucumber grower in Ames County, bar none."

"Guess that would be the case, all right."

"I know how people see you, Jake. You're a leader, someone who has his eye on the future. Someone who has a vision for agriculture in these parts."

"Suppose so," Jake said. "Suppose so." He stood up a little straighter.

"You let me know in a week or so, Jake. The deal can't hold much longer than that. I'm giving you about as good an arrangement as you'll find anywhere."

"Does sound that way. Does sound that way," Jake said quietly.

23

Closing Down

Andy Meyer didn't deserve the abuse the community dumped on him. Not only did the letters to the editor in the *Link Lake Gazette* take him to task for something he had no control over, but rumors began flying that high school kids had been using the basement of the pickle factory as a place to "make out," as one rather outspoken member of the Church of the Holy Redeemed said. Of course there was not one shred of truth to that, but it was one of those rumors that worked its way through the Link Lake Tap, made the rounds of the grist mill, and only a day or so later was a topic of conversation among the women shopping at the Mercantile.

The Monday after the Clayton auction Dewey John drove over to the pickle factory to talk with him about the spot-rot situation.

"Everybody's got it in for me," Andy said. He sat in the little office with the payroll records spread out in front of him, doing the work that Helen Swanson had done so well until her disappearance.

"Jake Stewart thinks I came down too hard on him, that I should have bought more of his spot-rot cucumbers. All the little kids with pickle patches hate me for drying up their source of money. Those old biddies from the Church of the Holy Redeemed are blaming me for what happened between the preacher and Helen. And now this rumor that I allowed high school kids to screw in the cellar—well, that's just a crock."

Andy, usually so mild-mannered, was showing some of his mettle.

"What should I do, Dewey?" he asked. "Should I write a letter to the editor giving my side of the story? I could do that."

"Don't know if it would help," Dewey said. "Usually these things blow over and people forget about them when some other piece of news comes along."

"Doesn't seem to be blowing over."

"Oh, sometimes it takes a little while."

On his way back to the office, Dewey John decided to write a short editorial about the matter, hoping it would put to rest some of the rumors and outright lies that were floating around Link Lake. He wrote:

INCIDENT AT THE PICKLE FACTORY

Our community has taken an incident that occurred at the local pickle factory and made a mountain out of what is surely a molehill. We know that Pastor Arthur Ketchum and Helen Swanson, both employees at the pickle factory, have come up missing. There is no evidence whatsoever that illicit parties have gone on in the pickle factory basement or that our high school students have been involved. It is hardly fair to blame Andy Meyer, the pickle factory manager, for any of this. Those who know Andy consider him a young man of the highest integrity—this is his fourth year managing the factory, and no one has but the highest praise for his work.

Some people also blame Andy for the spot-rot problem. That is absurd. People have blamed him for refusing to buy their infected cucumbers. Do they expect the H. H. Harlow Pickle Company to purchase a spoiled product?

We should all be thankful that the Harlow Pickle Company has a factory here, and that they have chosen an upstanding person in Andy Meyer to manage it.

The same day the newspaper came out with the editorial supporting Andy, J. W. Johnson pulled up to the pickle factory loading dock in his green pickup and slowly got out. He walked with his head down, big shoulders slumped. He stomped up the stairway and slowly walked to the office where Andy was working on the books.

"Hi there, Andy," he said in his gravely voice.

"Hi," Andy answered, looking up from the salting records. He didn't remember Johnson ever calling him Andy before. "What can I do for you?" Andy expected a tongue-lashing about the preacher affair and how it was blemishing the good reputation of H. H. Harlow. He thought Johnson would say something like, "What would Mother Harlow have to say about all these goings on?"

"I'm afraid I've got bad news, Andy," Johnson said. He had a kind of hangdog look about him, his eyes were watery, and his face was red.

"Bad news?" Andy responded.

"Yup, worst kind of news." Johnson was fiddling with his green cap with the little cucumber on it. "Don't even know how to say it."

"Well, just spit it out," Andy said. He had heard nothing but bad news for the past few weeks, and one more piece wasn't going to make much difference.

"Harlow is closing this factory when the season ends."

"They always close it at the end of the season."

"Well, this time it's for good. No more pickle factory in Link Lake. You are out of a job as manager."

"Why?" Andy said, too loudly. "The spot-rot problem? The preacher affair? Something else I did?"

"None of those things, Andy. Not one of those things."

"Well then, why?"

"It's economics. That's how young Harlow explained it to me. They can't afford to keep this factory and a bunch of other little ones going. They're closin' them all down and buildin' a big new pickle factory in Green Bay."

"What about all the farmers and their pickle patches? What about them?"

"Farmers will be offered contracts to grow cucumbers, as long as they agree to grow at least twenty acres. No more little cucumber patches."

"No more little ones? Why, we've had pickle patches in Ames County for thirty-five years," Andy said. "Maybe fifty years."

"That bastard Harlow can see nothin' but dollar signs. He's a son of a bitch. He's already holding Jake Stewart's feet to the fire, offerin' to keep him goin' with a loan Stewart will never be able to pay back. Makin' him put in fifty acres next year!"

This was the first Andy had heard about the deal Harlow had offered Jake Stewart. He thought about the sacks upon sacks of cucumbers that had come in from Jake's place, most of them rotted, rejected, sent back to spread on his drying fields.

"Know what else, Andy? He just up and fired me. Yesterday, when he was tellin' me all this, he finishes talking about closing the pickle factory and not takin' pickles from the small acreage growers, and then he says, as an afterthought, 'Oh, we're firin' all our district managers, too. We're going for a different approach to management.' The bastard just up and fires me without even takin' a breath, puts me in the same category as a little pickle patch. Gone."

"Well, I'm sorry to hear that," Andy said. "Sorry to hear about all this."

"Andy, I've got a big favor to ask," Johnson said, somewhat hesitantly.

"Yeah?" Andy, said, feeling a little wary.

"Suppose you could put in a good word for me with the Chicago Pickle Company in Redgranite? I applied for a job there today, and they said I needed some references. Harlow said he'd write a reference, but what in hell kind of reference can I expect from him? Bastard fired me, didn't he?"

"Suppose I can do that for you, J.W.," Andy said.

"I know we didn't get off on the right foot, Andy, and that I was a little hard on you at first. But you're a good man, a good manager, a damn good manager." Johnson's voice was tight.

"I'll put in a word for you," Andy said. He was wondering who would put in a word for him and what extra summer work he might find now that the pickle factory was no more.

"Thank you," Johnson said, grabbing Andy's hand and shaking it. "Thank you." Tears were streaming down the big man's face. "Thank you." He still held onto Andy's hand, continuing to shake it, apparently forgetting what he was doing. Then he let go, pulled a big green handkerchief from his pocket, and blew his nose. Remembering the main reason for his visit, he handed Andy a couple of big signs that explained the pickle factory closing and invited farmers to talk with a Harlow representative about signing a contract with them to plant twenty or more acres of cucumbers the following year. A Green Bay phone number and address were printed on the bottom of the poster.

Johnson's pickup slowly made its way up the driveway. Andy watched the little truck until it was out of sight. He felt sorry for blustery J. W. Johnson, but not nearly as sorry as he did for all the kids and their parents who depended on their pickle patches for a little extra money every year. At least half of these folks had already been dealt a bad hand when the factory had to refuse their cucumbers well before this season ended. But farmers were quite philosophical about these things. "Next year will be better." Always next year. It's a farmer's mantra. But there would be no next year for families with little pickle patches.

Andy's dad had grown a small cucumber patch for as long as Andy could remember and years before that as well. He wondered how his dad would take the news about the cucumber factory closing and Harlow insisting that they would buy only from growers who contracted for twenty or more acres, bought their seeds and fertilizers from them, and had them arrange for migrant help.

He and his father had talked about what they heard happened to Jake Stewart—how he was about to lose some of his land because he couldn't make mortgage payments, and how he was depending on cucumber money to bail him out. Andy knew his father wouldn't think much about the new arrangement Jake was making with the Harlow people, but then what was Jake to do? "Get in bed with the devil and you often have a hard time crawling out," his father would probably say.

When Andy got home that afternoon, he saw a letter in a blue envelope propped up on the kitchen table.

He picked it up and recognized Amy Stewart's handwriting. He had not heard from her since she wrote to him a few days after Link Lake Pickle Days.

Andy took out his pocketknife, opened the blade, and slit the envelope open. He pulled out and unfolded a sheet of perfumed paper.

"Dear Andy," he began reading.

24

What Next?

If ever a guy felt like eating crow, Dewey John did when Andy Meyer called and said that Harlow was permanently closing down the pickle factory in Link Lake and would no longer buy cucumbers from small acreage growers. The editorial he had written defending Harlow for both the spot-rot situation and the preacher debacle now seemed a huge mistake. He was going to be mighty embarrassed when people read about the factory closing.

He remembered what the owner of the paper said to him when he was first hired as editor: "Dewey, you've got to find the big story before you can write the little one; you've got to know what else is going on in the woods before you can write about the trees."

It had taken him a while to figure out what his new boss was talking about, but he had it right. He'd said, "If you're going to write about farms and farming, you'd better learn about rural communities, what holds them together and makes them work. You'd better study country people, what they're like and what keeps them going. And you'd better find who's trying to manipulate them."

Dewey wanted to get on the phone to young H. H. Harlow III and give him a piece of his mind—let him know what he was doing to the small family farms in Ames County. But then he reminded himself that he was a newspaperman and wasn't supposed to take sides, except in his editorials.

Andy had also told Dewey John about J. W. Johnson being fired. Dewey decided to give Johnson a call and get his take on the story. When he asked Johnson what he thought about Harlow's decision to close the pickle factory and fire the district managers, Johnson let loose a string of cuss words that you could hear all the way to Oshkosh. Johnson figured he had been wronged in every way. "That bastard Harlow didn't understand my job."

Dewey thanked him for his thoughts and hung up, shaking his head.

Sometimes one has to take the tiger by the tail, so Dewey John next called the Harlow Pickle Company phone number in Green Bay. He was put on hold for a few minutes, and then Mr. Henry H. Harlow III came on the line. Dewey told him he was with the *Link Lake Gazette* and wondered if Harlow had time to answer a few questions about the Harlow Company's recent decision.

"Sure," Harlow said. He sounded friendly enough. "Fire away."

"Why did you close the little pickle factory here in Link Lake? It's been here since the 1930s."

"Yes, it sure has. It's one of our oldest little factories—really just a salting station, you know; they don't do any processing beyond salting. It's just too out of date. The equipment is old. The salting tanks are worn out. It's not profitable to keep it going."

"Any other reasons for closing it?" The editor was fishing for whether or not the bad publicity about spot rot and the preacher affair had anything to do with the company's decision.

"No. It's all based on economics. We're building a new modern processing plant in Green Bay. We'll not only salt, but we'll make dills, slicers, pickles for the restaurant trade—and we even plan to make kosher dills. The demand is growing for kosher dill pickles, you know."

"When's your new plant opening?" John asked, trying to put some kind of positive spin on the story.

"We hope to be up and running in the spring, in plenty of time for next summer's processing season. I could arrange a special tour of the plant for you—I'll let you know when it's finished."

Dewey said he would enjoy a tour. He continued his questioning. "What about your decision to buy only from growers with twenty acres or more of cucumbers? You realize that farm kids with little cucumber patches depend on that money every summer."

"The board discussed that at length. It was a tough decision to make. It created a lot of disappointment, I'm sure."

"I'm afraid you don't know the half of it," Dewey replied, trying not to sound too angry.

"The quality coming from those little patches is too uneven—some growers do a good job, some don't. We've got to have a quality product, and we're just not getting consistent quality from the small cucumber patches."

What Dewey wanted to say was that Harlow didn't have any control over the small acreage farmers. What the company wanted was a smaller number of growers, all with contracts, like Jake Stewart. With a contract, farmers had to do exactly what the pickle company ordered them to do.

"What should I write about your decision? Do you have something you want to say to all these farmers and their kids with the little cucumber patches?"

"Yes, yes, I do. Tell them that H. H. Harlow regrets the decision we made to quit buying cucumbers from small patches. Tell them to consider growing at least twenty acres of cucumbers next year, and we'll be glad to do business with them."

"What about the spot-rot problem?" John asked.

"That was a temporary problem. A minor setback. We've got a good supply of disease-resistant seed ready for next year."

Again Dewey bit his tongue. He wanted to tell Mr. Henry H. Harlow III that spot rot had nearly destroyed Jake Stewart.

"Have you spoken to Andy Meyer, your factory manager here in Link Lake?" John asked.

"No, I haven't spoken to him, but I plan to do so soon. On my next trip out your way I'll be speaking to him."

"Does closing the pickle factory have anything to do with Andy?" John asked. He needed to know the answer.

"It has nothing to do with Andy whatsoever. We've always given him high marks. He is one of our better young managers."

"Thank you for your time," Dewey said and hung up. He had a story, a bigger story than spot rot and preacher shenanigans—a story on the same level as the closing of the Rose Hill school.

W<small>hen</small> Andy saw that the letter was from Amy, he thought about putting it away without reading further—the day had been lousy enough. But he was curious, so he read on. The letter was carefully written with a fountain pen, in Amy's characteristic handwriting—she was left-handed, so all the letters leaned a little to the left.

> Dear Andy,
>
> I've wanted to write for a long time, but I just haven't gotten up the nerve. Did my dad tell you that I'm quitting my job and

moving back to the farm? As you may know, he's run into some money problems because of the spot-rot disease. He needs someone to look after the books and see if we can get all this straightened out.

The guy I was going with turned out to be a real jerk, a city guy with only one thing on his mind, as it turned out.

Well, how are you? You've had a busy summer at the pickle factory, the way it sounds. Spot-rot problem seemed like a real mess. Dad never said much about how you were handling it. I suspect he had so many problems of his own he didn't notice. He's in pretty deep to the Harlow people.

You know, Andy, Dad always liked you, ever since you were a little kid and we were playing with your red wagon and you were hauling my dolls around. I think my mother took a picture—I'm sure it's around the house somewhere—of your wagon and my dolls. Since Mom died, Dad hasn't done much in the way of keeping the house in order. I'm sure the picture albums are there somewhere.

What I'm getting around to, and I know it's taking me awhile—could we get together sometime? I think we've got a lot to talk about, Andy. I'm sure you don't know how much I've missed you. But it's been awful not hearing from you, not talking with you.

I'll be home in a couple weeks—let me know when we can get together.

Love, Amy

Andy carefully folded the letter and shoved it back into his pocket. He ran his hands through his unruly hair, and then he rubbed his leg where he had been wounded. Days when the humidity was high, he was reminded of Korea—a memory he wished he could blot out. He walked out to the barn. He and his dad had things to talk about.

25

The Family Farm

Dewey John couldn't move past the anger he felt, which was mixed with considerable embarrassment. But he had learned a valuable lesson: be careful who you support before doing more research and learning the facts. You may regret your decision. He wrote the following editorial during the week of September 12, to appear the following Wednesday.

BIG BUSINESS AND FARMERS

By now most people have heard that the H. H. Harlow Pickle Company of Chicago is permanently closing their pickle factory in Link Lake. They plan to open a large, modern cucumber-processing plant in Green Bay. Starting next year the company will not buy cucumbers from a grower who does not have a contract with them. To obtain a contract, a farmer must agree to grow at least twenty acres of cucumbers and abide by Harlow's many rules. A farmer must buy seed and fertilizer from Harlow, plant when Harlow says to plant, and harvest when Harlow says to harvest. The farmer must employ migrant workers who have been recruited by Harlow, with a portion of the migrants' income going to Harlow.

The Harlow situation is but one example of what is happening in agriculture. The big meatpacking plants are contracting with farmers and giving them long lists of rules to follow; so are the big poultry-processing companies. Is this what the farmers in our state want? We don't think so. But many farmers see no other way. For them, the choice is to "sell their souls" to big business or get out of farming. Financially, the big agribusiness company may be a farmer's only choice.

It is a strange twist from the time when a farmer was his own boss, made his own decisions, and reaped the return on his efforts. Now a farmer makes few decisions, and the big agribusiness firm with which he has a contract makes most of the money.

We believe it is time for farmers to rise up and fight this trend, to reclaim their rightful place as family farmers.

Ever since Dewey John had moved to Link Lake, he'd been impressed with the small farms scattered throughout this part of central Wisconsin. None were especially prosperous, but these farmers raised their kids, sent them to school, and made enough money to pay their taxes and mortgage payments. The smart ones, and that included most of them, had made enough money during World War II to pay off the mortgages on their farms. Hog prices were good then; so were milk prices. After years of the Depression and then war, these farmers deserved to have things a little better.

Now, Harlow planned to close the pickle factory and pull the plug on small cucumber patches. *What next?* Dewey John wondered. He had covered stories of University of Wisconsin agricultural economists coming through town since he arrived in Link Lake in 1951. They preached bigger is better—bigger farms, bigger barns, bigger tractors, more cows, increased acres of crops. The university professors also pushed for big consolidated schools and the closing of one-room country schools. None of these "learned people" talked about the effects of these changes on rural communities.

Some of Dewey's newspaper friends, especially those in Madison, said he was trying to hold onto a dream, a bit of nostalgia, and the sooner he moved away from the notion of farming as "a way of life" to farming as "a business," the better off he would be. A friend from the journalism school in Madison who had read his recent editorial said Dewey John was holding back progress with his old-fashioned ideas.

He typed a quick reply.

Dear Tom,

So I'm holding back progress, am I? First, what in hell is progress? Is it progress when farm kids have to leave the land to find work? Is it progress when a farmer has to work night and day, plowing more acres and milking more cows, just so he can make ends meet?

Is it progress when farmers have to lick the shoes of the big company executives in order to stay in business, to sign contracts that take away nearly all their decision-making ability? Is that what you call progress?

I'd call what's happening out here in the hinterlands destruction. Blatant destruction of farm life as we have known it since the state was first settled in the 1840s and 1850s.

Don't you realize what we are giving up when we lose a family farm? It's a way of life, but so much more. We lose people who know the land and how to care for it, who know livestock and how to raise it, who know machinery and how to keep it operating, and who know what community means. That's what will be lost when these family farms disappear.

What about the businesses in town that depend on these farmers—the grist mills and feed dealers, the hardware stores and the lumberyards? What will happen to these small towns if all these businesses close?

Dewey John didn't hear back from his friend. He wasn't sure why. He wondered if his letter helped his friend think in a new direction or if Tom had dismissed his comments as those of a crackpot who was living in the past.

When Andy Meyer got to the barn, his dad was busy scattering feed in the concrete manger in front of the stanchions before allowing the cows into the barn for the afternoon milking. The barn's smells changed with the seasons. Summer included fresh lime spread in back of the cows mixing with the sweet scent of ground feed. The pleasant aromas of dried alfalfa, sweet and red clover, timothy, and brome grass in the haymows on the barn's second floor drifted into the lower reaches of the building where the cows were milked.

The horses, Frank and Claude, didn't come in the barn but pastured and grew fat and lazy as the summer work slowed. The Farmall H tractor did the heavy work on the farm these days.

"Hi, Andy," Isaac said when Andy pulled open the barn door and entered. Something about his dad's voice wasn't the same as usual.

"Something wrong, Pa?"

"Got a letter today from the Link Lake Cheese Factory. It's layin' up there by the milking machine pump."

Andy saw the brown envelope, picked it up, and removed the letter inside. It began:

Dear Link Lake Cheese Factory Patron:

Our board at its meeting last week voted to no longer accept milk from patrons who use ten-gallon cans. This ruling will go in effect over three years—we will no longer accept milk shipped in cans as of January 1, 1958. We are encouraging our patrons to purchase bulk cooling tanks as soon as possible.

We know this may be a burden for our producers with smaller

dairy herds, but to continue to ensure the quality of our product, we feel the decision is necessary. Handling milk cans is hard work for our milk haulers. Keeping these cans clean is also a challenge— we use enormous resources for can washing each day.

As a valued patron for many years, we know you will understand our need for progress. We stand ready to offer loans to those of you who wish to purchase a bulk tank. We have already made arrangements with a bulk tank company to provide tanks to our customers at a reduced rate.

Sincerely,
Oliver Sorensen
Manager, Link Lake Cheese Factory

"We can't afford no bulk tank, Andy, and I ain't about to take a loan from the cheese factory. Poor old Jake Stewart's all caught up in loans from the H. H. Harlow Company to the point that he may not crawl out of the hole he's in. Besides, where in hell would we put a bulk tank? We'd have to build a new milk house on one end of the barn. And then that bastard Sorensen at the cheese factory will want us to put in a pipeline milking machine—you know, the kind that pipes the milk directly from the cow to the bulk tank. Expect they'll offer loans for that too," Isaac continued, with a cynical edge to his voice. "You know what this is all about, don't you Andy?"

"I expect so, Pa," Andy said.

"It's all about driving us small farmers off the land. That's what it's about and I don't know what to do about it. Don't know what to do. It's a case of fighting them 'get bigger' bastards, joining 'em, or gettin' the hell out of the way. And you can't really fight 'em. You knock off one, and two more pop up in their place. It's just a bitch, what's going on in this country. Them big businesses jerking us little guys around, putting a collar around our necks and leading us like we was some anemic little city dog that ain't got enough gumption to even bark. Those of us who stay in farming are gonna be like that, Andy, like one of them little white dogs. I saw a tourist dragging one down Main Street the other day. Poor damn little dog could only yip; expect if it would bark it'd probably rupture itself. We're gonna be like that, Andy. Like that miserable little white dog with a red ribbon tied on its head."

"I don't think we're quite like little dogs yet," Andy said, chuckling. "But let me add another verse to that song you're singing."

"What's that?"

Andy told his father about the pickle factory closing, his being let go, and Harlow's decision to not buy any more cucumbers from small acreage growers.

Andy's father got red in the face when he heard the news. "One goddamn thing after another. I told you, them big companies are out to get us."

"Appears that way, Pa."

Father and son stood looking at each other, neither speaking for a moment.

"It's a bitch, ain't it, Andy? It's just a bitch what's going on. If we was to have a bulk tank, we'd have to milk at least thirty or forty cows to make it pay. If we had that many cows, we'd have to put an addition on the barn. We'd have to borrow money to do that, plus build a new milk house and buy a pipeline milking machine. Tell you the truth, Andy, I don't know what we should do. And now you tell me that we can't grow a pickle patch anymore, that Harlow won't buy our cucumbers."

"They'll buy them, but you got to grow at least twenty acres and have a contract with them."

"What they did to you, Andy, firing you on the spot, and now they expect me to sign a contract with them? To hell with them. To hell with that J. W. Johnson who was stomping around in our pickle patch like he owned the place."

"They fired Johnson, too."

"Well, that's good. He had it coming. He was a worthless pup. Could tell from the day I first saw him. A worthless pup. Sure wouldn't put you and Johnson in the same gunnysack, but sounds like Harlow did. Put you both in the same sack and dropped it in the river so's you'd drown together. That company turned out to be a bunch of bastards. Real bastards."

"Got a letter from Amy Stewart today," Andy said quietly.

"Saw the envelope. What'd she want?"

"Wants to talk."

"Talk, huh," a slow smile spread across Isaac Meyer's face.

"That's what she said. She also said she was coming home to help her dad on the farm, said Jake had gotten into some money problems."

"I guess we all know about Jake's problems don't we? He's a good example of what happens when you crawl in bed with the big guys."

"You don't know the half of it, Pa. According to Johnson, Harlow wants to loan Jake more money to put in more acres."

"More acres of rotten cukes?" Isaac sounded disbelieving. "I don't know what they're thinking."

"Maybe thinking they found an indentured servant in old Jake Stewart," Andy said.

Isaac shook his head.

"Amy quit her job at J. I. Case. Be here in a couple weeks."

"You gonna talk to her?"

"I don't know, Pa. With the pickle factory closing and me getting fired, Preacher running off with Helen, and now all this stuff from the cheese factory, I don't know what to think. Don't know what to do."

"Amy's a nice girl, Andy, in spite of her old man."

"I know that, Pa. But she dumped me for a guy who builds tractors. I'm just supposed to say, 'Hey, that's alright. Okay to have a fling with a tractor guy. Nothing wrong with that'?"

"Up to you to figure all that out, Andy."

"I know that, Pa." Andy grabbed a fork and headed for the straw stack outside the barn to gather up some straw for the calf pen.

That evening, not long after suppertime, the whistle on top of the fire station blew long and loud, summoning the Link Lake volunteer firefighters. The sound could be heard for miles out of town, as it was a clear night with no breeze.

The local firefighters rushed to the firehouse and climbed on the ancient fire truck, which they'd somehow gotten to run again after it died during the Pickle Parade. The truck chugged down Main Street, a huge cloud of black smoke billowing from its exhaust pipe as it wheezed and backfired.

The fire was at the end of Main Street, a huge towering blaze that sent gray smoke high into the air. The firefighters immediately unwrapped their fire hose and turned on the water from the truck's tank—there were no fire hydrants in the Village of Link Lake. Why would you have one when your town is next to a lake?

But the firefighters sprayed not one drop of water on the structure because it was so hopelessly engulfed. They wet down the ground around it so the dry grass wouldn't burn.

The "Leaning Pickle of Link Lake" was on fire. One of the volunteer firefighters noticed an empty gasoline can nearby, but he kicked it aside and didn't tell anyone that the fire had likely been set. No one needed to know. Nearly everyone in town rushed out to watch the fire demolish the leaning monstrosity. The big pickle stood for the H. H. Harlow Company, which had paid for its construction. Some people cheered, others clapped—showing their hatred toward the H. H. Harlow Company and what it had done to their community.

The owner of the Link Lake Tap hauled over a keg of beer and tapped it. "Free beer for everyone," he announced, and the adults lined up.

Joe Sagwell from Sagwell's Drug Store and Soda Fountain toted over ice cream and offered free double-dip cones to the kids.

Someone saw musicians Albert Olson, T. J. Jones, and Louie Pixley in the crowd and suggested they go home and fetch their instruments. They were soon back from their farms and playing the "Beer Barrel Polka." "Roll out the barrel. We'll have a barrel of fun!" Everyone sang and danced as the big leaning pickle began collapsing on itself, sending sparks high into the air. Some later said the flames were seen as far away as Willow River. The party continued long after the leaning pickle was but a bed of coals, glowing red in the night.

26

Decision Time

Friday, September 16, would be the Link Lake Pickle Factory's last day of operation. This was about the usual closing date for the factory, although because of the spot-rot problem, few cucumbers had been delivered during the past few days. Andy had laid off Quarter Mile and Blackie a couple of weeks ago, and he let Agnes go just yesterday.

Dewey John stopped by that afternoon. He wanted to do a story about the place, to let people know that this little cucumber-processing plant had been an important part of the community's life for many years. He didn't want people to just forget about it. This happened sometimes when a bachelor farmer died and left no heirs. The poor guy got a little stone in the Link Lake Cemetery with his name, birth date, and date of death, and that was it. In a year or two people forgot about him, almost like he'd never lived at all, hadn't been an important part of the community. One of the things Dewey John tried to do through the newspaper was make sure people and important events weren't forgotten.

Dewey didn't want people to forget the pickle factory, either. He wanted them to remember how that fading gray building had brought money, and much more, to the community. Beyond the financial help it provided farm families, the old factory had more stories than cucumbers associated with it. Stories provided the core for memories; they deserved to be recorded and passed on from generation to generation.

And, good newsman that he was, Dewey wanted an update on the preacher affair. He wondered whether Andy Meyer had heard anything more about what happened and where the preacher and the bookkeeper had ended up.

Andy was working alone in the office when Dewey arrived. He was fussing over some final reports for Harlow that were spread across the old scarred desk.

"Hi, Andy," Dewey called as he climbed the steps to the receiving platform and proceeded to the little office with its open door.

"How you doing, Dewey?" Andy said, looking up from the reports and putting down his pencil.

"Came to take one more look at the place," Dewey said.

"Just look around to your heart's content. Gonna miss this place. Expect the whole community will miss it."

Dewey John liked Andy and appreciated his leadership style. He was impressed with how Andy had handled the preacher affair, the factory closing, and his own dismissal as factory manager. And he respected how Andy had handled the women from the Church of the Holy Redeemed. They couldn't let up on him and continued to blame him for ruining the life of their beloved, beyond-reproach preacher. They called Andy everything from the devil's servant to one who condoned debauchery. With such unfounded criticism, Dewey certainly would have overlooked a little more anger on Andy's part, and maybe even a "Why don't you old pious fussbudgets just go to hell" statement or two. But Andy never did anything of the kind. And he had handled the factory closing the same, quiet way. He simply put up Harlow's sign explaining why, and he didn't whine because he had lost his job.

Andy and Dewey John walked around the deserted factory together, past the old cucumber sorter that had seen better days but with a little tinkering could continue to operate at some other place. Andy mentioned that Harlow would probably move the sorter out to Jake Stewart's farm, now that Jake planned to grow fifty acres of cucumbers next year.

They walked among the filled pickle vats, the slightly acidic smell of fermenting cucumbers still hanging in the air. They walked by the salt bin, now nearly empty. Andy thought about the fight between Blackie and Quarter Mile, but he didn't bring it up. They climbed down the steps and walked around the outside of the building, peering through the little door to the basement, near where Andy had caught the preacher and the bookkeeper together.

"Lots of stories here, Dewey. Lots of stories in just the four summers I worked here," Andy said.

"Shame to see her close. Darn shame. Be just like closing down the grist mill, or that sawmill there across the tracks, or pulling out the railroad," Dewey said. He was making notes on the papers on his clipboard.

"Hard to figure out what's going on in the country," Andy said. "What's a young guy like me supposed to do? Pa'd never admit it, but seems it was easier for him. All he had to do was take over where his pa left off. And that's what he did. Took over from Grandpa and farmed much as Grandpa did. Of course Grandpa never had electricity, a tractor, or a milking machine."

They stopped and stood in the shade of the big old building. "What do you think of the cheese factory's decision not to buy milk from farmers who use milk cans?" Andy asked.

"All part of what's happening to farmers," Dewey said.

"We'll either have to buy more cows or get out of the dairy business. I'm not sure Pa will buy more cows. It all costs money, lots of money, and Pa isn't one to do much borrowing. He saw what happened to poor old Jake Stewart when the spot rot got his cucumbers."

"Yeah, it's true. Borrowing money gets more farmers into trouble than about anything else," Dewey agreed.

"Know what happened yesterday, Dewey? Darndest thing. Henry Harlow III himself stopped by. The big boss. Never met him before. Heard a lot about him, but never saw him before."

"What'd he want? I just talked with him on the phone the other day. He want to apologize for closing the plant and firing you?" Dewey said with a cynical laugh.

"Nah, can you believe it? He wants to hire me—offered me a job!"

"Hire you?"

"Yup. He said I was one of their up-and-coming young managers and he offered me a job in Green Bay to work at their new plant."

"Well, that's something. Offered you a job after firing you."

"He really never fired me. Johnson said they were closing the pickle factory here, and I wouldn't have a job."

"Sounds like firing to me. No pickle factory, no job."

"Anyway, Mr. Henry Harlow III says to me, 'Andy, how'd you like to be production manager at our new plant in Green Bay?' I suspect I just stood there looking stupid, because that was about the last thing I expected to come out of his mouth. Then he says, 'We'll pay you $6,000 a year.' After a little while I say, 'How much did you say that was?' And he repeats it, '$6,000 a year, with two weeks' vacation and sick leave.'

"You know, I have never had a vacation or sick leave. Pa and Ma never had a vacation, ever. Farmers don't take vacations when there are cows to milk. So I say to Mr. Henry Harlow III, who stands there in his fancy dress pants, shiny black shoes, and a going to church shirt and tie, 'I'll have to think it over.'"

"That's one fancy job offer," Dewey managed to blurt out. "I didn't know of anybody pulling down that kind of money in Link Lake."

"Expect not," Andy said.

"You going to take the job?" Dewey asked, looking Andy in the eye.

"I don't know. I just don't know. Pa wants me to take over the farm; I know he does, even with all the changes that are coming down the road. And I think I could make a go of it, too."

"You still dating Jake Stewart's girl?"

"Not really. She's been off working in Racine, you know. For J. I. Case. Dumped me back in July. Sent me a Dear John letter."

"Jeez, what got into her?" Dewey said.

"Some guy in the tractor plant got her attention."

"Yup, know how that goes."

"Wrote to me the other day and said she dropped the tractor guy and wants to talk. Said she was coming back to work with her dad."

"You gonna talk to her?"

"Don't know. Old Jake isn't very subtle about his daughter and her future. It's pretty clear that he wants me to marry her and take over his big operation. I suppose I could make it work, too. But don't know if I want to."

"Get the girl, get the farm. Sounds like a deal to me," John said.

"Maybe. But I just can't see big-stakes farming. I saw Jake suffering through the summer."

"So what are you gonna do? Work with your dad, take the job in Green Bay, or marry the girl and work out a deal with her old man?"

"I don't know. I just don't know," Andy said.

27

Another Mystery

Dewey John walked into the newspaper office the morning after he visited the pickle factory. He heard the phone ringing and expected the call was from someone asking if he thought it might freeze tonight. Dewey didn't know why people thought he'd know about the weather. It had rained all night, and a cold front was blowing through. And it could freeze. Here it was only September 17, and much of the corn was not yet ripe. An early season frost would really cap it off for the farmers who had lost their cucumber crops to disease and now could lose their corn crops as well. Early autumn weather in central Wisconsin was unpredictable, always had been, probably always would be. After endless days of warm, summery weather, just like that, a cold rain will blow in from the northwest, the sky will clear, and the temperature will drop like a lead sinker in a barrel of water.

"This here is Marshal Quick," the voice on the other end of the line said. "Just got a call from Tiny Urso, one of Jake Stewart's hired men. He's the big guy who stutters—took him forever but he finally spit out that Jake has come up missing. You wanna ride out there with me? Might be a story."

Dewey said he knew who Tiny Urso was and that he'd be ready when the marshal stopped by the newspaper office. He grabbed up his Rolleiflex camera, several rolls of 120 Tri-X film, and his clipboard.

They drove out to Jake Stewart's farm with the marshal doing most of the talking. He jabbered on about kids who'd just gotten their drivers' licenses and were driving up and down Main Street on Saturday nights.

"They drive down by the grist mill, turn around, and then head on north by the Standalone Cemetery, turn around, and do it again. They ain't speeding, just creating a nuisance, especially for the tavern-goers who wanna cross the street. These guys with half a buzz on, they're the ones who think I oughta fine these kids for driving on Main Street."

"Yup, I've noticed the kids on Saturday nights, too," Dewey said. But he wasn't thinking about kids; he was thinking about what they'd find at Jake's farm. He wondered if Jake had up and run away. It wouldn't be like him, though. But he'd really gotten himself in a financial mess.

The marshal went on. "Yeah, those same guys that complain about the kids driving on Main Street, they're the ones who would really snort if I stopped them for driving drunk. I stopped old Jeremy Aldrich the other night, and he started yelling like a stuck pig. He stunk like a brewery. Said I had no right to stop him. He reminded me that his taxes were payin' my salary. I agreed that he probably paid some of my salary and then I gave him a ticket. He was mad as hell. Said he was gonna bring it up with the mayor. I said, 'Go ahead.' Some days this job can be a bitch."

"Sounds that way," Dewey said, not really listening to the marshal's litany, but more concerned about Jake Stewart.

"You know this hired man, Urso?" the marshal asked, finally changing the subject.

"Know who he is, that's about all," Dewey said.

"Well he's got quite a story. He's a big guy, maybe six-and-half-feet tall and weighing right around two-fifty, and you know he's got a stuttering problem."

"Don't think I've ever seen him."

"And I bet you didn't know what happened one day at the Link Lake Cooperative Store."

"No, I didn't hear that story," Dewey answered, now well aware he was going to get all the details.

"Well, one day the co-op hires a guy who also stutters. Tiny stops at the cooperative to pick up something, and the two stutterers, neither knowing the other has a speech problem, face each other.

"'Wh-wh-wh-what c-c-can I do for you,' the fellow at the cooperative asks.

"'I-I-I-I n-n-n-n-need some block salt,' says Tiny.

"'You-you-you-you-you mockin' me?' the feed store fellow says. He's a big man, too, but not Tiny's size.

"'N-n-n-n-no,' says Tiny.

"'Wa-w-w-w-well it sounds like it to m-m-m-me.'

"The two of them almost get into a fight before they figure out that they each got the same problem. They then shake hands, and they've been good friends ever since. It's something to hear the two of them carry on a conversation, really something."

"I'll bet it is," Dewey said. He could see the driveway into the Stewart yard a short distance ahead.

Everything looked normal when they pulled in. Since Jake's wife died, the flowerbeds alongside the house were empty and the lawn was seldom mowed. The barnyard fence needed a new coat of paint, and the barn did, too, for that matter. It was obvious that Jake had more things on his mind than keeping his farmstead neat and tidy.

Dewey noticed that Jake's big Buick was parked by the house and his pickup stood by the tractor shed, so he could tell Jake didn't drive off in one of his own vehicles.

Tiny Urso stood by the barn waving his arms, directing them that way. Marshal Quick turned off the engine of the squad car, adjusted his hat, and hitched up his belt with the .38 revolver hanging on the side. John gathered up his camera and clipboard.

"I-I-I-I can't find Jake," Tiny stammered. "He-he-he-he-he's missing."

"Have you checked at the house?" the marshal asked Tiny matter-of-factly.

"Y-y-y-yeah, I did."

"Not there, huh?"

"N-n-n-no, not there." Tiny was perspiring and obviously quite upset.

"Did you look in the barn?"

"Y-y-y-yeah, I did."

"Not there either?"

"N-n-n-not there either."

"Where do you suppose he is?"

"D-d-d-d-don't know. It's-it's-it's-it's why I-I-I-I-I called."

"Well, we better have a look around, then," the marshal said, "make sure he's not here someplace before we start assuming that

208

he's somewhere else." Dewey had always marveled at Marshal Quick's great sense of logic, and this was a classic example. If a fellow isn't here, then he must be someplace else—a line of thinking that started with the assumption that everybody must be someplace. The marshal often reminded Dewey of that when people came up missing. He remembered when he and the marshal had discussed the disappearance of the preacher and the pickle factory bookkeeper. The marshal had wanted Dewey to quote him in the paper: "Everbody's got to be someplace, no getting around it. If they ain't here, then they're somewhere else."

That's how his mind worked. Everything was pretty much black and white, right or wrong, and simple as hell. His was not a complicated world.

They looked in the haymow of the barn, recently filled with baled hay. They looked through the lower part of the barn, where the cows were milked each morning and night. They looked in the tractor shed and the granary.

"Anything unusual happening around here the last day or so?" the marshal asked Tiny Urso.

"N-n-no, c-c-c-can't think of anything."

"Any visitors?"

"O-o-o-only the trucker from Ha-ha-Harlow Pickle Company. Br-br-brought a load of fer-fer-fertilizer yesterday afternoon. B-b-b-big load."

"Where'd he put it?"

"O-o-over there." Tiny pointed to a large new metal shed that Jake had put up earlier that spring.

They walked over to the shed, and Tiny pulled open the big sliding door. Immediately they saw a huge pile of hundred-pound 3-12-12 fertilizer sacks spilled all over the floor. Each sack was green and had the words "H. H. Harlow" emblazed on its side in large print.

"Da-da-damn pile tipped over," Tiny stammered.

"Sure did," the marshal replied, once more restating the obvious.

"Can't say as I've ever seen this much fertilizer in one pile," Dewey said, as he walked around the tangled mess of fertilizer sacks scattered all over the shed floor.

"'B-b-bout fifteen ton," Tiny said.

"Well, I don't see any sign of Jake in here. Anyplace else you can think to look?" the marshal asked. He cracked his knuckles, hitched up his belt, and fingered the handle of his pistol.

"W-w-w-what's that?" Tiny asked, pointing to something sticking out from under the fallen stack of fertilizer sacks.

"Looks like an old shoe," the marshal replied.

Dewey and the marshal pulled away a couple of sacks of fertilizer and discovered a leg attached to the shoe.

"Oh-oh-oh," was all that Tiny could say as the three of them uncovered the body of Jake Stewart. He had been crushed when the big pile of H. H. Harlow fertilizer sacks tumbled on top of him.

Dewey took several pictures, trying to avoid Jake's face, which was a horrible sight, all black and blue and crushed on one side.

"Gotta call the coroner," Marshal Quick said. "Coroner's got to have a look at this. The house open?"

Tiny Urso shook his head up and down. He looked like he was going to throw up.

Dewey John followed the marshal to the house. While the marshal was calling the coroner, Dewey couldn't help but see a short, handwritten letter on the table, near some dirty dishes. The letter read:

Another Mystery

Dear Dad,

I'm coming home. I'm sorry you're having all these problems and I think I can help. I quit my job at J. I. Case today, and I'll be home next week.

I miss you, Dad.

Love, Amy

28

Remembering Jake

In extra large print, the headline of the *Link Lake Gazette* read, "Prominent Farm Leader Dies in Freak Accident." A two-column story followed. "Jake Stewart, 65, was found Saturday under a large pile of fertilizer bags on his rural Link Lake farm." The story went on to detail the events of Stewart's death, including a half-page photo of the toppled fertilizer bags with a visibly upset Stewart employee, Tiny Urso, standing nearby.

Some wags in Link Lake thought it was suicide, as many people suspected Jake had financial problems, especially since the spot-rot disease wiped out his thirty acres of cucumbers. But the coroner's report was clear and quoted in the newspaper. "Cause of death: farm accident."

The news story concluded, "The funeral will be held at the Link Lake Methodist Church on Friday at 11:00 a.m. with internment at the Link Lake Cemetery following the services. Lunch will be served by the women of the church following the internment."

Dewey John also wrote an editorial.

Remembering Jake

JAKE STEWART REMEMBERED

Not everyone always agreed with Jake Stewart, but everyone respected him as a leader in this part of Wisconsin. When farmers still planted an acre or two of cucumbers, Jake was willing to take a risk and plant thirty acres. When numerous farmers believed that a country-school education was good enough for their children, Jake argued long and hard that rural children deserved an education comparable to children in urban areas.

When many farmers were skeptical of the university's College of Agriculture and its teachings, Jake Stewart embraced it. He became a close friend of the county extension agent and also with a College of Agriculture cucumber researcher, who spent many hours at the Stewart farm.

We will all remember Jake Stewart for his sincerity, his love of farming, his competitive nature, and his willingness to try something new. He is survived by his daughter, Amy, who until recently was employed by the J. I. Case Company in Racine.

Of course the discussion at the grist mill, in the saloons, at Korman's restaurant, at the cheese factory, and wherever people gathered was about Jake Stewart's farm and what was going to happen to it.

"Heard that Lake National Bank's gonna take it all," one farmer from the east side of town proclaimed, as he sipped a glass of beer at the Link Lake Tap. "Yup, that's what them banks do. You get in trouble and they come down on you. Take your land away faster'n you can say, 'This was once my granddaddy's farm.' Them damn bankers just don't care. Miserable bunch they are."

Fellow next to him agreed. "Yes sirree, that's likely what's gonna happen. Bank'll take over the farm, then sell it. Wonder's who's gonna buy it? Big place. Thousand acres, you know."

"City guys, that's who. City guys are buyin' up all the vacant land around here. Buyin' it for a summer place and a place to hunt," another regular at the bar chimed in. He had just drained his glass and held it up to the bartender for a refill.

"Know what I heard?" a local livestock hauler chimed in. "I heard old Jake's daughter, Amy, is taking over the place and running it just like her old man did."

"Where'd ya hear that?"

"Heard it over in Willow River when I was delivering pigs this morning. Everybody's talking about Jake's farm, even over there. Nobody in these parts has a farm as big as old Jake Stewart's. Fellow I talked with knew Amy, said he went to high school with her. 'She's a smart one,' the fellow said."

The stories began spreading around, most of them not built on a shred of truth.

On Wednesday afternoon, a big Buick pulled into the Meyer farmstead and stopped near the kitchen door; Andy, Isaac, and Mary were just about to sit down for supper before Andy and his dad would go out to the barn to do the evening milking.

"Looks like old Jake's car," Isaac said. "Yup, it is, and it's Amy driving. Poor thing, wonder how she's taking all this?"

Amy, wearing a dark dress, walked up to the kitchen door and knocked lightly.

"Come in, Amy. Come in," Mary said. "It's good to see you. We're just so sorry about your dad. So sorry. Everybody's sorry. Such a shock. Are you hungry? We'll set another place."

"Thank you," Amy said quietly. Her eyes were red from crying.

Andy got up quickly and found a chair on the far side of the kitchen.

"Here, Amy," Andy said. "Sit down." He held the chair for her.

"Thank you, Andy," she said, a slight smile on her lips. "It's so good to see you," she said in a near whisper as she sat down.

Andy stood holding Amy's chair, trying to think of the right words to say.

"I have a favor," Amy said.

"Anything at all, Amy. Anything at all," Isaac said.

"Would you . . ." Amy hesitated a bit as if to collect herself. "Would you and Andy be pallbearers at Pa's funeral?"

"Of course we will. Be proud to do it," Isaac said. "I guess I knew Jake longer than just about anybody around here. Expect he was the first kid I ever played with. Walked to school with him for eight years, too. We had good times, your pa and me," Isaac said.

"I'll ask some of the other neighbors, too. And maybe Ole Olson from the mill in town," Amy said.

"Nobody will turn you down, Amy. Not at a time like this," Isaac said. "Yup, Jake and I go back a long time. Chased girls together. Bet you didn't know that your pa once had his eye on Mary here. Bet you didn't know that?"

"Now Isaac, Amy doesn't want to hear about that sort of thing," Mary interrupted. She had gotten up to tend to the supper on the stove.

"Then we watched each other farm. I'd start plantin' corn, and then Jake would plant his. He'd start makin' hay, and then I'd start. We always were lookin' to see what the other guy was doin' and when he was doin' it. Kind of fun, it was. Those years were fun. You and Andy were just little tykes, then. Playin' in the sand together. Playin' farmin'. That's what the two of you were doin'. While your pa and me were plantin' corn, you and Andy were makin' little rows of corn in the sand box out back of the house."

Amy's shoulders began to shake. Then she buried her face in her hands and burst into tears. Mary was quickly at her side.

"It's going to work out fine, Amy. Crying can be a good thing sometimes. Remembering good times helps everyone."

Andy, not sure what to do, got up and went to the window that looked out toward the barn. He knew he should say something to help Amy, but what? What could he say? What could he do?

When supper was over, Amy said, "Thank you so much. That was delicious as always."

"It's the least we could do, Amy," Isaac said.

Mary gave Amy a big hug. "Anytime you want to talk, Amy, you just stop by. These are tough times."

Andy walked with Amy to the car. He opened the door for her, but rather than climb into the Buick, she put both arms around Andy and kissed him hard on the lips.

"I've missed you so much," she said. "I love you, Andy."

"I've missed you, too," Andy said, a bit surprised. He put his arms around her and held her tight for a few moments.

Andy stood watching the Buick go down the driveway and onto the country road.

He made his way out to the barn to do the evening milking, his mind a muddle of tangled thoughts.

29

Funeral

The first cars began arriving at the Link Lake Methodist Church by ten o'clock, a full hour before Jake's funeral was to begin. Marshal Justin Quick, wearing a freshly pressed white shirt and his ever-present cowboy hat, was on hand to help with the parking. He was standing in the street and pointing toward the big field back of the church where cars were lining up. The marshal "howdied" each driver, and welcomed those people he didn't recognize to Link Lake. He followed the "Howdy" with a "Nice day, wouldn't you say?" He repeated the litany over and over, as each car arrived.

A rainstorm had come through the area on Thursday and took with it the haze and humidity of summer. Friday had dawned cool and bright. It was a good day for a funeral. It was a good day for just about anything.

The Methodist church was soon filled to capacity with people standing in the back and lined up on the steps, hoping to catch a phrase or two of the minister's message. The organ music and the singing of "Nearer My God to Thee" and "What a Friend We Have in Jesus" rolled through the little sanctuary and out the front door to the people standing on the steps.

Soon the service was over, and the people on the steps stood back as the wooden casket and its six pallbearers slowly moved toward the open doors of the hearse. Amy walked with the pastor and Mary Meyer directly behind the casket. Two dozen red roses were lying on the casket, with the words, "From your loving daughter, Amy."

Amy was crying softly as she slowly moved down the steep church steps. Everyone stood quietly as the pallbearers shoved the casket into the back of the hearse and quietly latched the vehicle's door.

Meanwhile, Marshal Quick had been organizing the funeral procession that would drive down Link Lake's Main Street, and then out of town to Link Lake Cemetery. The marshal later said that the procession was the largest he had ever been in charge of, with more than forty cars. Someone else thought there were only twenty-five, which still made it the longest funeral procession Link Lake folks had ever known.

The cars, all with their lights on, moved slowly out of town: Marshal Quick's squad car first, with the red light flashing, then the hearse, followed by the mortuary's big black Oldsmobile. Amy, Mary, and the pastor rode in the Oldsmobile, followed by pallbearers in another car.

The procession was slowed down when it came upon a farmer with a big load of second-crop hay. The farmer's wagon was pulled by a team of workhorses. He was going right down the middle of the narrow road. The farmer was obviously more interested in saving his hay than attending Jake's funeral. (Jake hadn't used horses for ten years.) There was no way for the farmer to pull over to the side of the road without tipping his load of hay, so he continued on, even though he could see cars backed up to the top of the hill leading into Link Lake. The marshal didn't know whether he should turn on his siren and risk scaring the horses and causing a runaway or just follow along behind, hoping the farmer would turn off into a nearby farmyard. Of course some of the people toward the end of the procession, especially those from out of town, didn't know about the load of hay and were becoming a bit impatient.

Finally, the hearse pulled into the cemetery, followed by the entire procession. The marshal, usually quite thorough about these matters, hadn't planned how to handle the parking at the cemetery. Cars were parked here and there and everywhere and along both sides of the county road.

Soon the crowd, more than a hundred mourners, gathered around the gravesite.

"Ashes to ashes, dust to dust," the minister intoned as the casket was slowly lowered into the grave.

People began returning to their cars, trying to follow Marshal Quick's muddled instructions about how to exit the cemetery.

Amy and Andy remained at the gravesite, their heads bowed. They didn't see the man in a black suit standing in the shade of an old burr oak tree near the road. The man came out of the shadows as Amy and Andy walked toward the car, where Mary and Isaac were waiting for them.

"It's Amos Caldwell, the banker," Andy whispered to Amy.

"Hello, Andy," the banker said. Andy nodded.

"Hello, Amy. I was so sorry to hear about your loss."

"Thank you," Amy said. "Thank you very much."

"Your father was an important person in our community; he will be missed."

"Yes, I surely miss him."

"Amy, we have some business to discuss with you. I'm wondering if you could stop by the bank, say next Monday at eleven?"

"Sure," Amy said.

"Again my heartfelt condolences to you. I am sorry for your loss. See you on Monday, then."

The banker briskly walked away.

"Well, the nerve of that old bastard," Andy muttered.

The local gravedigger was shoveling dirt into the grave, slowly, meticulously, one shovelful after the other. A red-tailed hawk soared overhead, its wings nearly motionless.

Andy agreed to accompany Amy to her meeting at the bank. Amy had begun sorting through her father's records and discovered that his debts were much more than she even imagined. She wasn't looking forward to meeting with Amos Caldwell.

When Andy stopped by Stewart's to pick up Amy, he noticed a big H. H. Harlow truck parked near the metal shed where Jake had died. Workers were loading fertilizer.

"See Harlow wasted no time in picking up the fertilizer," Andy said.

"Guess it's theirs to take. Pa hadn't paid for it. So good of you to come along, Andy." She grabbed his hand and squeezed it.

They drove slowly toward Link Lake, past the cucumber fields that had been plowed under once the spot-rot disease had been discovered, past acres of cornfields where the plants, more than head high, had tasseled and were forming ears, past potato fields with dark green plants in neatly cultivated rows as far as a person could see. All of this was a part of the Stewart farm, clearly the largest enterprise in the area. They traveled more than a mile without losing sight of Stewart holdings.

"It's beautiful," Amy said. "Just beautiful. Pa would have been so pleased to see how the crops are doing this year. Besides the cucumbers, that is."

"Good growing year," Andy said. "Rains came at the right time."

"Mr. Caldwell is waiting in his office," the woman behind the counter said to Amy and Andy by way of greeting when they entered the lobby. Andy noticed that she looked especially glum this morning. Counting money all your life must have that affect on a person, he surmised.

Amos Caldwell, his bald head shining, stood up from behind his desk.

"Thank you so much for coming in this morning, Amy," Caldwell said. "I know you must be very busy."

A man sitting off to the side in the thick-carpeted office stood up and extended his hand to Amy. "I'm Henry Harlow, from the H. H. Harlow Company," the man said. He turned and shook Andy's hand as well. "How are you, Andy," he said.

"I'm just fine," Andy replied.

The banker hesitated for a moment, cleared this throat, and said, "Andy, I'm afraid you will have to leave. This is a private meeting with Amy."

Andy stood, but Amy reached for him and grabbed his arm.

"Andy is my fiancée," Amy said, looking Caldwell in the eye. "He stays."

"Uh, I didn't know," Caldwell stammered. "Congratulations."

Amy glanced at Andy and smiled. Andy, looking surprised, smiled back.

"All right then, let's get down to business," Caldwell said. The banker had a huge stack of papers in front of him.

"Your father was in some financial difficulty when he died," Caldwell said matter-of-factly.

"I know," Amy said.

"Without going into all the details, Mr. Harlow and I have been doing some figuring."

Andy eased closer to the banker's desk.

"We'd like to save us all some legal bills, and frankly I don't want to foreclose on your property," Caldwell said. "By doing what we're proposing, no one will have to know how deep in debt your father really was."

"What are you driving at, Amos?" Andy said, leaning forward, his elbows on the desk.

"Mr. Harlow here has agreed to buy your pa's property, the land, the equipment, the buildings, everything," the banker said, looking at Amy.

"The entire operation?" Andy said, surprised.

"All of it," Caldwell answered. It's the only way to clean up what is frankly quite a financial and legal mess.

"What does Amy get out of this?" Andy asked, staring at Henry Harlow.

"We're offering fifty dollars an acre for the land," Harlow said. "That's a fair price, especially for this many acres. That totals fifty thousand dollars. That amount of money will pay off the bank and cover what your dad owed us and several other people."

"And Amy, what does she get?" Andy repeated.

"Well," Harlow said, looking down at his notepad. "With the title transfer fees and such other expenses taken out, Amy will get about five thousand dollars, the way we figure it."

Amy was quiet for a moment, staring down at her hands. "What about the house?" she asked.

"The buildings go with the deal, but we will allow you to live in the house until January 1."

"Is that it?" Andy said.

"I'm afraid that's the best we can offer, under the circumstances. Let us know in a week if we have a deal."

They shook hands all around and Andy and Amy returned to their car.

"So, when did we get engaged?" Andy smiled as he looked toward Amy.

"About a half hour ago," Amy said as she turned and kissed her new husband-to-be.

They drove quietly for a while. "What should I do?" Amy asked as she turned to Andy.

"About getting married?" Andy teased.

"No, silly, about the farm. My mind is swirling. I never thought we'd lose the home place."

"Sounds like Harlow is willing to buy it. Different from losing the farm. And nobody would find out how deep in debt your pa really was."

"I expect you're right, Andy. And five thousand dollars is a considerable sum."

"More than I've ever seen in one place," Andy said.

30

H. H. Harlow

Less than two weeks after the bank, H. H. Harlow, and Amy Stewart closed the deal on the Stewart farm, the *Link Lake Gazette* carried a front-page story.

> The H. H. Harlow Company of Chicago has purchased the thousand-acre Jake Stewart farm in rural Link Lake for an undisclosed sum of money. Henry Harlow, company representative, said the company has several anticipated uses for the land: "We plan to establish an experimental farm where we, in cooperation with the College of Agriculture in Madison, will test new varieties of cucumbers, green beans, field peas, sweet corn, and potatoes. We also plan to grow about two hundred acres of cucumbers for our new processing plant in Green Bay. Additionally, we'll establish a cucumber receiving station on the property, for area cucumber growers with Harlow contracts. Finally, we plan to remodel the old Stewart house and use it as a conference and training center. Vegetable experts and growers from around the world will come to Link Lake to learn what's new in vegetable growing."
>
> The company plans to employ about twenty-five people year-round, and of course more in the summer. Harlow announced that they have already hired Carlos Rodríguez, formerly of Texas, to be in charge of field operations. Rodríguez will live on the former Stewart property in a new home the company is building for him

and his family. Tiny Urso, longtime Stewart employee, will continue in Harlow's employ.

The community is planning a special ribbon-cutting ceremony for the Harlow company at a date to be announced.

In the same issue of the paper, this brief announcement appeared.

Andrew I. Meyer, 25, of rural Link Lake and Amy E. Stewart, 23, previously of Racine, Wisconsin, announce their engagement to be married. Mr. Meyer farms at Rural Route One, Link Lake, and is the former summer manager of the local H. H. Harlow cucumber salting station. Miss. Stewart was previously employed by the J. I. Case Company. A Christmas wedding is planned.

Although the farmers in the Link Lake community were still smarting from Harlow's decision to only buy cucumbers from those willing to grow twenty acres or more, local merchants looked forward to increased business from all the activities the Harlow Company was planning on the Stewart farm. With the announcement in the paper, the H. H. Harlow Company was viewed in two lights in the community. Small family farm owners detested and did not trust the company. Business people saw more dollars in their cash registers. Almost everyone agreed that the H. H. Harlow Company would certainly put little Link Lake on the map if they carried out all their plans.

Isaac and Mary Meyer were elated when they learned of their son's engagement to Amy Stewart. But they were devastated to learn how serious Jake Stewart's financial situation had been. "I'll bet old Jake didn't even know he had all that debt," Isaac said.

Isaac and Mary invited Amy to share Thanksgiving dinner with them. Amy had been busy cleaning out her family's old house, sorting through the attic, deciding what items she wanted to keep and what should be thrown. As difficult as the job was, both physically and emotionally, she was discovering the history of her family, from the time when her great grandfather bought the place. She found neatly written letters, notes, and documents showing that her great grandfather, Silas Stewart, had purchased the original quarter section of land in 1855 for $1.25 an acre. She burst into tears when she realized the land had been in her family for one hundred years, and now it was gone. She felt like she had let her great grandfather down by selling the land and removing the Stewart name after a century of ownership. Had she acted too quickly in accepting H. H. Harlow's offer? Could she have done something to save the place?

Amy shared some of this information, including her second thoughts, at the dinner table where they had gathered to eat roast turkey and all the trimmings and feast on Mary Meyer's pumpkin pie, one of her specialties.

"It's done, Amy," Isaac said quietly. "There comes a time to move on. To set a new direction and let history rest."

"But it's so hard." Amy looked like she was going to cry.

"Change is never easy. Never easy for anybody. I hate it myself," Isaac confessed. "I like to keep things just like they've been. It's so much more comfortable."

He took another bite of pumpkin pie.

"Talking about changing and moving on, Ma and I have an announcement to make."

Neither Andy nor Amy knew what to expect, except that maybe it had something to do with their upcoming marriage.

"Andy, you know your ma has always wanted to move to town when we got older. Well, we've been talking about that the past several weeks, and we've made a decision."

"You're moving to town?" Andy asked, too loudly.

"Yup, your ma and I are gonna look for a little house in Link Lake."

"But . . . but . . . what about the farm?" Andy was both surprised and flustered by what he was hearing.

"Oh, we'll sell the cows, probably next month," Isaac said quietly.

"Sell the cows?"

"We'll use the money from the cows to buy a house. Should even have a little money left over."

"But what about the farm?" Andy asked. He was clearly beside himself. Amy sat quietly, with a puzzled look on her face. This was not like the Isaac Meyer she had known over the years. Isaac was always careful and deliberate, sometimes taking a year to make a decision.

"Oh, didn't I say?" Isaac said, with a little smile spreading across his face. Mary was also smiling.

"Ma and I are giving the farm to you and Amy as a wedding present."

"Giving us the farm!" Andy said.

"Figured it was the right thing to do. Figured the two of you would come up with a way of making a living off these 160 acres."

"But Pa, how are you and Ma going to live without the income from milking cows?"

"Remember, Andy, I'm past sixty-five now. I get a social security check each month," Isaac said proudly.

"Thank you, thank you," Amy said as she put her arms around her future father-in-law and kissed him on the cheek. Isaac patted Amy on the arm.

31

Mystery Solved

It took only a week for Isaac to find a buyer for his cows, and at a higher price than he had hoped for. He had milked cows since he was a small boy, and he was a bit surprised at how difficult it was to see the last animal walk up the ramp into the cattle truck. It's one thing to talk about change and how to face it, it's quite another to experience change first hand, especially when it involves animals that you have loved and cared for since they were little calves.

Soon the truck rolled out of the driveway and disappeared down the road. Isaac had out his big red handkerchief and was blowing his nose. "Cattle stirred up lots of dust," he said.

That evening, there were no cows to milk at the Meyer farm. No hay to toss down from the haymow. No straw bedding to spread. No calves to feed. Andy and his dad walked out to the barn after supper, as they had done for as long as Andy could re-member. They pulled the barn door open and rather than sense the warmth associated with a building filled with animals, they noticed the barn was cold for the first time. Andy and his dad stood back of where the cows once stood, neither saying anything, and then they went back to the house. Isaac flipped on his favor-ite new television show, *Gunsmoke,* for it was Saturday night.

Mystery Solved

A week later, on December 17, Andy and Amy helped his folks move into their new place in Link Lake, a little bungalow that had a view of the lake and was within easy walking distance of most businesses.

Amy and Andy moved furniture from the Stewart place to what would become their new home and even bought a few new pieces with a little of the money Amy had gotten from Harlow. By the time of their wedding on Christmas Day, the Meyer house had taken on a new look. It was now Andy and Amy's home. Amy wanted it to be special yet have hints of the history associated with both their families.

The days flew by for the young couple as they worked on their plans for doing something quite different from what either of their fathers had done. Andy worked at transforming the cattle barn into a retail store where he hoped they could sell jams and jellies, pickles of various kinds, and fresh homegrown vegetables. Of course, all would be grown on their farm and other smaller farms in the community.

Both he and Amy spent days sweeping and scrubbing the upper part of the barn, where hay had been stored for the cattle. They planned to make this huge space available for wedding receptions, polka dances, and anniversary and birthday parties.

Finding a name for their operation proved more difficult than they had anticipated. They scrapped several early attempts, "Meyer-Stewart Vegetable Farm," "Homegrown Vegetable Farm," and several other equally bad names. Finally they agreed on "Rose Hill Farm Market," after the country school that they had both attended.

On a sunny day in mid-March, with the winter's snow melted and the frost out of the ground, a crew of workers from the H. H.

229

Harlow Company set in posts and nailed up boards to enclose the entire thousand-acre former Stewart farm with a white board fence. Every few hundred yards, the workers erected signs that read, "H. H. Harlow Experimental Farms. No Trespassing."

That same day, Amy and Andy sat at their kitchen table with seed catalogs spread in front of them. They were making a list of vegetables that they believed would attract people to their farm—people who wanted to buy homegrown vegetables that were sold where they were grown. Or, people would have the option of picking the vegetables themselves—green beans, peas, onions, sweet corn, beets, rutabagas, potatoes, and of course cucumbers. Amy also wanted to grow pumpkins for jack-o-lanterns.

Additionally, the young couple listed several varieties of strawberries and raspberries they planned to grow, along with several kinds of apple trees. It would take a few years for the various fruits to become established, especially the apples.

Andy had just returned from the mailbox when the phone rang. Amy answered it.

"It's for you, Andy."

"Hello," Andy said. He listened for a few moments. "I don't work for Harlow anymore." He listened some more. "Ok, I'll meet you at the pickle factory."

"What was that?" Amy inquired. She had begun preparing lunch on the new gas range they had recently purchased.

"Marshal Quick wants me to meet him at the pickle factory. Can't image why. I'd better get down there."

When Andy arrived at the old pickle factory, which looked even more tired and worn since last fall, when it had closed for the last time, he noticed a special railway tank car on the siding near the back door of the building. Nothing unusual about this. Each year about this time, Harlow sent workers to each of its salting stations to transfer the cured cucumbers and brine to a railroad tank car, which hauled the cucumbers to their main processing plant in Chicago.

Marshal Quick stood at the door, his hands on his hips and his big cowboy hat pulled down low.

"Men found something in one of the tanks," Quick said. "Something mighty interesting."

"What?" Andy asked.

"Couple of dead bodies. Pickled bodies." The marshal smirked when he said it.

"Do you know who?"

"Yeah, I do. No doubt about who they are. No doubt at all."

"Well, who are they?"

"It's that runaway preacher and your bookkeeper. That's who."

"Preacher and Helen?"

"That's what I said."

"What were they doing in a pickle vat?"

"I was hoping you could tell me."

"How am I supposed to know why they turned up in a pickle vat?"

"You ran this place didn't you? You were the one in charge."

"Yes, I was in charge."

"Did you know about this last summer and keep it to yourself. Are you keeping information from the law?"

"What?" Andy said, incredulously.

"You heard me," the marshal said. He rested his hand on the butt end of his pistol.

Just then Dewey John arrived, notebook in hand.

"Hi, Andy," Dewey said. "What's going on here?"

"They found Preacher and Helen in a pickle vat."

"What? When?"

"About an hour ago, when they began moving pickles into that tanker car."

"Anybody know what happened?" Dewey asked. He turned to the marshal, his pad and pencil at the ready. "Marshal, what do you know about this?"

The marshal cleared his throat. "This morning, employees of the H. H. Harlow Pickle Company of Chicago discovered two bodies in a pickle vat. They were entirely covered with cucumbers."

"They were the Preacher and Helen, right? The ones that came up missing last summer?" Dewey asked.

"That information is correct," the marshal said.

"Do you know what happened to them?"

"I have been interrogating Mr. Andrew Meyer, former manager of the pickle factory about that matter. The county coroner is also doing an autopsy to determine the cause of death."

"Do you have any theories about what might have happened?" Dewey asked. He continued to make notes on his pad.

"As a sworn lawman, I only deal with evidence, not theories," Marshal Quick said.

"I see," Dewey said, smiling. "Andy what do you think happened?"

The newspaperman and Andy walked over to the number-two vat where the bodies were found. The bodies had been removed earlier, as had most of the cucumbers. They leaned over the edge of the wooden vat and glanced inside. There were still three or four feet of fermented cucumbers floating in the eight-foot-tall tank. The sides were still slippery from the brine. The pungent smell of cucumbers and salt brine filled the air.

"Got any theories, Andy?" Dewey asked again.

"Well, here's my take on what happened. Flimsy wooden boards covered those pickle vats. They were breaking regularly. And sometimes, when you piled something on the edge of one, the cover would tip and dump whatever was on top into the vat. Then the cover'd flop back into place and nobody'd know what happened. I think that's what happened to the preacher and Helen that night. Maybe Helen and Preacher snuck back into the pickle factory after it closed for the day. Helen had a key. They decided to, . . . well, enjoy each other on top of the number-two vat and fell in when the cover tipped. They drowned because there was nobody around in the middle of the night to hear their cries for help. The sides were too slippery to crawl out," Andy said.

"Sounds reasonable to me," Dewey said. "What do you think, Marshal?"

"Can't rule out murder, never can rule out murder. In fact probably a good chance they were killed," the marshal said. "Next step is to question their families, see if they had any enemies."

The following item ran in the Gazette that week:

RUNAWAY PREACHER AND BOOKKEEPER
FOUND IN PICKLE VAT

Workers from the Henry H. Harlow Pickle Company on Monday found the bodies of the Reverend Arthur Ketchum, 35, and Helen Swanson, 30, in a pickle vat at the Link Lake Pickle Factory. Justin Quick, village marshal, believes they were murdered and dumped into the pickle vat to hide the bodies. However, Prudence Words-worthy, a longtime member of the Church of the Holy Redeemed, said, "I believe our beloved pastor was so overwrought with guilt from his wrongdoings that he and the harlot, Helen Swanson, committed suicide by leaping into the vat." No suicide note was found, however.

Preacher Ketchum's wife, Ethel, was so overcome with grief that she was unable to give a statement.

Andy Meyer, summer manager of the pickle factory, believes the two were in the pickle factory one night and fell into the pickle vat and drowned.

Marshal Quick, offering some historical perspective on the tragedy, said, "The last killing in Link Lake took place in 1904, when Marshal Maynard 'Shorty' Lightfoot confronted bank robbers who blew the safe at the Link Lake National Bank. Lightfoot tracked the robbers out of town and accidentally stumbled onto them in the big woods north of Link Lake. He ordered them to halt, and when they didn't he said he would shoot. When he pulled back the hammer on his revolver, it accidentally fired, killing one of the robbers."

The investigation of the pickle-vat murders continues, with Marshal Quick in charge.

"I anticipate this inquiry will take a long, long time," Quick said.

32

Barn Dance

Andy Meyer got up early this June morning, as the sun was rising. After a couple of days of welcome rain, raindrops still hung on the little cucumber plants as he worked his way down the row, hoeing out weeds. He was enjoying the quiet. He heard a mourning dove call in the distance, and sitting on a nearby fence post, a meadowlark was singing its spring song. A slight breeze rustled the needles of the row of majestic white pines that bordered the pickle patch, making a soft, soothing sound.

Andy's father, who nearly every day drove out to the farm from Link Lake, would arrive soon. Isaac, as he had done for years, would hitch the old gelding, Claude, to a one-row cultivator. The two of them, the old plodding draft horse and the old farmer, were much alike. They both moved slowly and methodically, but they got the job done. Above all, both horse and man enjoyed what they were doing. Isaac would work until noon today, turn Claude out to pasture, and then return to his home in Link Lake.

At the end of the row, Andy stopped to rest. He gazed across his fields of potatoes, strawberries, raspberries, and pumpkins. He looked at the long rows of carrots, lettuce, beets, broccoli, onions, cabbage, sweet corn, and squash—all crops Amy and he planned to sell at their new Rose Hill Farm Market.

How everything had changed from a year ago, Andy thought. At that time, he was sure he would be milking cows and working part-time in the pickle factory for years to come. But now the cows were sold, the factory was closed, and his dad and mother had moved to town. And—he was a married man. As he stood looking across the many rows of vegetables, old worries about making big changes returned. He knew how to farm like his father and his grandfather before him. He knew how to care for cows, how to make hay and grow corn, and how to raise cucumbers. Running a farmer's market and processing fruits and vegetables was new to him. Andy worried about change, even wondered about the goodness of it. Wouldn't life be easier without everything changing, when you could depend on things being the same, day after day, month after month, year after year?

He had talked to Amy about this, probably too many times. Change had been one of the topics where the young couple had had the most disagreement. She pushing forward, he always holding back.

Before this past year, Andy hadn't thought much about the big agribusiness firms that were marching out into the countryside, contracting with farmers to grow chickens, hogs, beef cattle, vegetables. When Harlow issued its contract edict, it struck him. Andy made up his mind that he would not sign such a contract, and because of what had happened to her father, it wasn't difficult to convince Amy. He and Amy wanted to keep control of their farming operation. To farm as they wanted to farm, to grow as little or as much of any crop as they wanted, and to sell directly to those who wanted fresh produce. They wanted to make their own decisions without somebody in a suit looking over their shoulder.

Andy and Amy had big dreams for their new ideas about farming. They had worked hard since April, tilling the ground and planting row upon row of vegetables. They had planted several hundred apple trees—McIntosh, Cortland, Jonathan, and Red Delicious. It would be several years before their new orchard would bear fruit, but they enjoyed planning for the future.

Andy noticed a red car coming down the country road, then turning into their driveway and stopping by the house. Traveling salesmen interested in selling special cow feed had mostly stopped coming, once they heard the Meyers had sold their cows. So Andy wondered who this could be. Amy was working in her flower garden in front of the house. She stood up when the man approached and then pointed to where Andy worked in the pickle patch.

As the man came closer Andy saw that he was tall and thin, and wore khaki trousers.

"You Andy Meyer?" the man inquired. He spoke softly.

"I am," Andy answered.

"Name is Hopkins, George Hopkins," he extended his hand to Andy. "Got some good-looking cucumber plants."

"We try," Andy said. He wondered what the fellow wanted to sell.

"Heard that you were planning to process these vegetables here on the farm and sell them at your farm store." He made a sweeping motion that went beyond the pickle patch to include the other vegetable fields.

"That's right. We'll make dill pickles, sweet pickles, pickle relish, sliced pickles. We'll sell jams and jellies, canned sauerkraut, pickled beets—about any homegrown product you might think of, and, of course, we're selling fresh vegetables, too."

"Believe you're the first around here to do this," Hopkins said.

"Probably so." Andy was becoming more curious about what the fellow wanted.

"I may be able to you help you out."

"Oh, you wanna hoe? Think I've got another hoe down in the shed," Andy said, smiling.

"Nah, I did my share of hoeing when I was a kid. My dad had a vegetable farm near Kenosha."

"So how you gonna help me out?" Andy said, wanting to get back to his hoeing.

"Well, my company represents gift shops and grocery stores all over the Midwest," Hopkins said.

"What's that got to do with me?"

"It would work like this. The excess product that you have, beyond what you can sell in your store, we'll distribute for you. I'm talking about the processed stuff, of course: dill pickles, jams, jellies, canned sauerkraut, pickled beets, that sort of thing."

"What do you get out of the deal?" Andy asked.

Hopkins smiled. He'd heard about Andy's father and how closely he kept track of his business, especially where his money went.

"We take a small percentage," Hopkins said. "And you get your "Rose Hill Farm" name in gift shops and grocery stores all over the Midwest."

"Amy and I'll have to talk about this. These kinds of decisions we make together."

"Want to help out if I can. Story of what you and your wife are doing has gotten around—don't know if you are aware of that."

Barn Dance

"I've heard so," Andy said. "But like my pa always says, 'Believe only half of what you hear and be highly suspect of the rest.'"

"Will you give it some thought?" Hopkins handed Andy his business card.

"We'll do that," Andy said. "And thanks for stopping by."

"Good luck to you and your wife," Hopkins said as he shook Andy's hand and walked off across the sandy field.

Andy quit hoeing at noon. The big open house for the Rose Hill Farm Market was planned for this evening and they still had some cleanup to do. They had invited all their neighbors, as well as the businesspeople from town. The open house included a potluck supper and then a polka dance in the hayloft of the barn, which had hosted two wedding receptions so far this June.

That afternoon Amy and Andy polished the display cases and dusted in all the corners of their new store on the ground floor of the barn. The cases prominently displayed strawberry jam and jelly, both with the new Rose Hill Farm label that featured a wild rose with the lettering around it. They'd bought the strawberries from a neighbor, because their strawberry plants wouldn't begin bearing fruit until next year. Another neighbor, Barbara Jenks, worked with Amy in their new commercial kitchen — the former milk house — to make the jam and jelly.

The display case also featured freshly cut leaf lettuce, baby beets, new red potatoes, big red radishes, and bunches of dark green broccoli, all from Andy and Amy's fields.

Andy's parents came out in mid-afternoon and helped with final preparations — setting up planks on sawhorses for the food, hauling chairs from the Link Lake Methodist Church, and putting up a sign by the road showing people where they should park.

Dewey John was the first to arrive for the "Big Party," as he referred to it. He wanted photos of Andy and Amy standing by their new big road sign. No one could miss the huge wild rose, surrounded by the words "Rose Hill Farm Market" and, in smaller print, "Pick your own fruits and vegetables."

Dewey toured the kitchen and the store, taking photos and asking questions. The earthy smell of fresh vegetables mixed with the sweet smell of newly made jams and jellies. Dewey walked to the hayloft, where the polka dance would be held.

"You've done a lot of work here," Dewey said as he glanced around the vast expanse of what had been the hay storage area in the old barn. He saw the wooden beams, twelve inches by twelve inches and many feet long that held up the barn. The wooden floor had been scrubbed until it shone.

Soon the neighbors from near and far began arriving, carrying hot dishes, cakes, pies, potato salad, sandwiches of many kinds, baked beans, bowls of fresh strawberries, three-bean salads, and Jell-O (green, red, yellow with shredded carrot). The food table was crowded with plates, platters, and bowls by the time people began lining up to eat.

Pat Patterson, his wife, and their gaggle of red-haired children came. So did Mr. and Mrs. Oscar Wilson, the John Korleskis, Iris Clayton, and Floyd Jenks and his wife. The pickle factory crew from last summer came: Blackie Antonelli; Quarter Mile Sweet, who was to be a sophomore at the university in Madison; Agnes Swarsinski, still cracking jokes; and even George Roberts, who had once more returned from the "cure" in Oshkosh. J. W. Johnson, Andy's former boss at H. H. Harlow, even showed up. "Got me a job at the Link Lake Mercantile," he said proudly. "Doin' everythin' from cuttin' meat to waitin' on customers."

Barn Dance

To Andy's pleasant surprise, Carlos Rodríguez and his family, now living year-round on the Harlow property in their new house, came. Mrs. Rodríguez was proudly showing off her new, plump-cheeked baby boy to everyone.

Ole Olson from the mill came, as did the undertaker, John Dobrey, and his wife, driving his big black Oldsmobile funeral car. And of course the little polka band came: Albert Olson the banjo player, Thomas John Jones the fiddler, and Louie Pixley with his concertina. They brought along their wives and children.

There were many more. People were interested in what Andy and Amy were attempting, especially the small farmers in the area. They all wanted to wish the young couple well in their attempt to transform what since 1890 had been a dairy farm into something different.

With the meal finished, and the cleanup completed, Andy invited everyone to the hayloft, where the little polka band was tuning up. The barn was lighted with antique kerosene lanterns that cast a soft yellow glow as the light reflected off of the old wood. Andy thanked everyone for coming and hoped they were having a good time.

Amy then took the floor: "Thank you all so much for helping us launch our new venture. Your being here means a lot to us. We appreciate your support; we'll need lots of it as we go along." Then she added, "But let's never forget that besides all the hard work, there should be a fun side to farming. Now let's all have some fun."

With that the band began playing an old-time waltz. Andy and Amy led off, dancing on a wooden floor that once had tons of hay dragged across it. The big wooden beams cast interesting shadows on the floor.

Others joined the young couple, and soon the old haymow floor was crowded with dancers. After the waltz, the band immediately swung into an old tune with a polka beat. "The old gray mare, she ain't what she used to be, ain't what she used to be, ain't what she used to be." The band sang the words and was soon joined by the dancers as they hopped around the floor.

The dancing went on into the night. Polkas, waltzes, circle two-steps. People dancing who hadn't danced in years. Old people dancing who had difficulty walking. Young people dancing, getting acquainted with each other, smiling. Little kids on the dance floor, trying to mimic the older folks, attempting to waltz and polka, but not quite understanding the steps. Fathers dancing with daughters. Sons dancing with mothers. Husbands with two left feet hauled out on the floor by their wives. Men dancing who only knew the beat of a two-cylinder John Deere tractor.

The double set of big barn doors was open, allowing the night air to cool the dancers. The sounds of the party rolled down the country road and across the fields and through the valleys, like a gentle summer breeze.

At about eleven o'clock, Andy noticed Marshal Quick's squad car coming down the road, its red light flashing. The marshal parked his car across the driveway, and the red light continued to rotate.

The marshal walked to the barn, his big white hat pulled nearly down to his ears.

"I'm looking for Mr. Andy Meyer," the marshal said in his most official voice.

"I'm over here," Andy said, waving his arm. "Welcome to our party."

"Mr. Meyer," the marshal said, "I am not here for a party. I am here on official business." He touched his hand to the ever-present pistol at his side.

"What official business at this time of night?"

"I have just received a complaint about this gathering."

"A what?" Andy said.

"A complaint."

"About what?"

"You are creating a disturbance. You are making too much noise, and all these cars are blocking the road." The marshal made a sweeping motion with his arm in the direction of the cars that were parked on both sides of the road.

"Who complained?"

"I'm not at liberty to say."

"Well, what am I supposed to do?" Andy asked.

"Tell the band to quit playing, so the people will go home."

"Quit playing so the people will go home?"

"That's what I said. Either you tell them, or I'll tell them."

"You tell them," Andy said. "You tell them to quit playing."

"Well, I will," the marshal said, pulling down his hat and adjusting his gun belt.

The marshal marched across the crowded floor; several polka dancers nearly ran into him before he reached the bandstand. The threesome had just finished playing a polka and were deciding on their next tune.

"Hello, Marshal. Do you have a request?" Albert Olson asked. He rested his banjo on his lap.

"You'll have to stop playin'," the marshal said.

"I don't think we know that one . . . never even heard of it," Olson said, smiling.

"You gotta stop playin'," the marshal said. He was not smiling.

"What?" Olson said, wondering if he'd heard correctly.

"The band must stop playin'."

"Who says so?" Olson asked.

"I say so," the marshal huffed.

"All right then, we'll stop," Olson said.

The dancers parted and the marshal strutted across the floor without looking back. When he got to his car, he turned off the red light and drove slowly into the night, in the opposite direction from the Harlow farm.

The band members had gathered around the lemonade cooler.

"What do we do now?" Andy asked Albert Olson.

"We start playing again. He didn't say how long we should stop."

Back at the bandstand, Louie Pixley said, "How about the 'Beer Barrel Polka'?"

The band began playing a louder than usual version of the tune, with all the dancers joining in the singing. The sound tumbled down the country road and through the open windows of the nearby Harlow Research and Conference Center where an international team of plant breeders was holding a late night session.

"What kind of music is that?" a noted horticulturist asked, as he tried to concentrate on the research paper he was presenting to the group.

"The local marshal is taking care of it," a Harlow representative replied.

Back at their farm, Andy and Amy stood off to the side, watching their friends dance.

"Sure have been a lot of changes this past year," Andy said.

"It's one thing we can count on," Amy said.

"I guess change isn't too bad, as long as some things stay the same," Andy said, smiling.

"Speaking of change," Amy said, "do you think Andy Jr. will like Rose Hill Farm Pickles?"

"Who?"

"Andy Jr.," Amy said quietly.

Andy looked at Amy and smiled.

Author's Note

I managed the H. J. Heinz cucumber salting station in Wild Rose, Wisconsin, during the summers of 1952–1955. This story is fiction but is loosely based on my experiences during those years. The characters are all fictional. There was no H. H. Harlow Pickle Company, no Rose Hill School, no Church of the Holy Redeemed, and no *Link Lake Gazette.*

In the 1950s, cucumbers were a popular cash crop on many central Wisconsin farms, including the one where I grew up. Cucumber growing especially fit farmers with several children, as they would help with the hoeing and especially with the picking, which was hard, hot, and back-breaking work. These pickle patches were tiny by today's standards, some only a quarter acre or so in size.

As the fields got larger, migrant workers, whom many called Mexicans even though almost all of them were American citizens from Texas, came to central Wisconsin in July. They worked in the cucumber fields until September, when most of them returned to Texas, so their children could go to school. One year when my father grew two acres of cucumbers, a migrant family, who lived at a neighboring farm, helped us with the picking.

The migrants, by and large, got along well in the community. Most could speak English. They bought their groceries at the local grocery stores. The owner of the Wild Rose Mercantile Store, Arnol Roberts, took some Spanish courses—of course, his business increased once the migrants knew he spoke some Spanish. Many migrants attended the Catholic church in Wautoma, which had a special Spanish mass.

The migrants attended the free outdoor movies on Tuesday night in Wild Rose, sitting on the benches next to the locals. They bought supplies at the hardware stores and purchased clothing at the clothing stores. There were few complaints from either locals or migrants. Most of the farmers, including myself, had never seen a dark-skinned person before the migrants arrived. Nor had we heard anyone speaking Spanish. We were, of course, accustomed to hearing German, Polish, or perhaps Norwegian spoken, but Spanish sounded different.

By today's standards, the housing provided for the migrants was deplorable. They lived in former sheds and other farm outbuildings. They had electricity, but no indoor plumbing or running water. In the 1950s, the majority of the farmers in central Wisconsin had gotten electricity only recently. Many of the farmers did not yet have indoor plumbing or running water in their own farmhouses.

Migrant workers had been coming to Wisconsin starting in the early 1900s, when they worked in the sugar beet fields. By the 1950s, most of them were helping harvest seasonal crops such as cherries (Door County) and cucumbers (central Wisconsin). The number of migrants working in the state peaked at about 15,000 in 1955.

By the 1960s, most of the small cucumber acreages had disappeared. Cucumber processors such as H. J. Heinz; Libby, McNeil and Libby; Redgranite Pickle Company; and the Chicago Pickle Company began contracting with farmers growing larger acreages. By this time, some of the larger growers had begun installing irrigation equipment that increased the per-acre production and led to more uniform, well-developed cucumbers. Nearly all the small cucumber salting stations in Wisconsin closed. The big companies trucked fresh cucumbers directly to their large processing plants in Green Bay and out of state.

Picking cucumbers is one of the few farm operations that has essentially eluded technology. No one has invented a mechanical picker that can harvest the crop without destroying the vines. For maximum production, a cucumber plant must be picked many times during the weeks it is producing—as many as fifteen or more times—and by hand. Today in central Wisconsin, migrant workers still do nearly all the cucumber handwork.

From the 1950s through the 1970s, Wisconsin passed a series of laws that helped protect migrant workers from exploitation. A 1977 law began regulating migrant housing, job contracts, minimum wages, and transportation. It also created the Governor's Migrant Labor Council, which made sure that that the provisions of the 1977 law were followed.